Listen Up,
GIRLFRIENDS!

Lessons on Life from the Queen of Advice

Listen Up, GIRLFRIENDS!

MOTHER LOVE
with Connie Church

St. Martin's Press
New York

Design by Junie Lee

ISBN 0-312-11995-X

First edition: May 1995

10 9 8 7 6 5 4 3 2 1

This book is dedicated, in loving memory, to my mother, Shirley Anne Hart, who was my teacher, my nemesis, and, most importantly, my *best* Girlfriend. I glory in your spunk!

ACKNOWLEDGMENTS

I want to thank God for blessing me with the talent to do anything.

My love and abiding affection for my husband Kennedy and my masterpiece, our son, Jahmal, who still made me do my wifing and mommying while writing this book.

A special thanks to my editor, Jennifer Enderlin, for thinking I could make a great book. And to her mother Maureen for encouraging her to go for it.

To my writer, Connie Church, who has become my friend and confidante. You will always be my Girlfriend and I want the world to know that you are truly, truly special because you are very special to me.

Thanks to my managers at the Suchin Company who have hung in there with me through it all.

And a collective Mother Love hug and thank-you to all my relatives, friends, and fans who through the years have touched my life. And a very special thank-you to all my Girlfriends.

I love you all.

CONTENTS

Okay, Girlfriends! This is your special time with Mother Love so listen up!

INTRODUCTION

*It's amazing to me that we can lick a little doodad, put it on
a letter, and it can get to anywhere in the world . . . but we
can't keep our relationships together.*
—Mother Love

❤   ❤   ❤

*L*isten up, Girlfriends!

Mother Love is here to tell you how to love and be
loved.

To tell you how to take care of yourself and other
people.

To tell you how to keep your family and other relationships together.

This is a book for all you Girlfriends. I don't care if
you are married, dying to get married, wish you weren't
married, have children, don't want any children, are working or trying to work—or just trying to figure out what you
have to do; what needs to be done to make your life right.

I'm here to tell you about the sacrifices (and you will
suffer), the choices, and the changes that you're gonna
have to make if you want to draw love into your life and
make your space a better place. And, oh Lord, if you're

anything like me, you've been making some bad decisions and ridiculous choices that have done nothing but cause you misery.

But as my mother used to say, "Baby, if you don't screw it up how you gonna know if you can fix it up? How are you gonna know what kind of backbone you have? How are you going to know what you can endure, live with, and deal with if you don't screw it up first?"

I have screwed up so much in my life. This is why I believe I am qualified to tell other Girlfriends—actually advise them, "If you do this, this will happen. If you don't do this then that will happen. And, if you do it that way, then you can expect this."

I don't want you to make the same tired mistakes that we've all been making for years. Girlfriends, it's time for a change!

There are no "color lines" here. I've written this book to connect us as women, whether it be as wives, mothers, sisters, aunties, daughters, grandmothers, and, above all, as Girlfriends. Each of us is special, but the thread that weaves us together is the never-ending list of our common experiences.

I've listened to so many of you tell me how you can't talk to your mother, can't find a good man, don't know what to do in a relationship, that all men are just dogs but you want babies, and you want this and you want that. . . .

Well, Girlfriend, what are *you* willing to do to make sure this happens? And don't you be rollin' your eyes and sucking your teeth and telling me stuff like, "Well, I don't want to do too much of nothing, because Fred just got finished with me and I hate them all!"

When your problem is with a man, first I have to ask,

"Where'd you meet that dunderhead?" I'd think twice before going back to that same place.

Now I've got to advise you, your attitude is the very reason that booty of yours doesn't have a decent man right now. For as many bad ones there are out there, there are plenty of good ones, too.

I know, because I've been there. I've been kicked around, worn down, misused, broke, busted and disgusted, and kicked to the curb, where I was promptly left for the garbageman on Tuesday. But I have also been treated like a true queen—to the point that all "he" needed to do to quench his thirst was drink a quart of my dirty bathwater!

Girlfriend, what you've got to understand is that attitude, emotion, and responsibility are all rolled up into one state of being. And you have to do your part. If you are not willing to sacrifice, compromise, and forgive, then you can forget about having any kind of positive relationship with anything or anybody—and this includes your dog. Period. Nobody said this would be easy, but it can be done. And after spending twenty-three years with the same man, eighteen years of motherhood, and seventeen years in the entertainment industry, I'm living proof.

When it comes to work and trying to make ends meet, whether you're a Welfare recipient or plagued by money problems, you can get out from under it. We all need some help every now and then, but Welfare ain't a job.

I was on Welfare until I realized that poverty was not going to suit me. It was not going to work. I could not live the kind of life I like, and that I was used to living, on $216 a month. Heck, I spend that on my "drawers" alone—and I wear big underwear!

Conversely, money ain't the whole show. Yeah, I

know, we all like having that cash to flash! And we all know that plastic is fantastic! But ultimately it's not that the things are so important; it's about what you do with what you have to create a quality life.

Girlfriend, you deserve a good man.

Girlfriend, you deserve a good place to live.

Girlfriend, you deserve a job that you like.

And, Girlfriend, you deserve as many babies as you can responsibly care for.

Never forget, Girlfriend, that if things are bad in any area of your life, you can always begin again. Sometimes your only choice is to make a radical change. I have started my life over half a dozen times, moving from city to city and place to place with nothing.

I came to California with two suitcases. Period. And coming to Hollywood, where everything is blond and tiny, was really difficult because I am a woman, I am a large woman, and I am a large, Black woman who doesn't have a problem with who she is.

The entertainment business can be very frustrating. I've been known to speak my mind from time to time. During one particularly difficult day I stood up and announced to some of these show-biz folks: "I ain't perfect, this is what I'm gonna do, and this is what I'm about. Mother Love has got an ego the size of Texas and it developed long before I showed up in Hollywood. I know who I am, where I am, where I'm going, and what I'm doing. I give an honest day's work for an honest day's pay. Don't mess with me!"

Well, they just went, "Damn! Okay. All right."

Truly, I try to treat people the way I want to be treated. But I know how to be mean. I can put the itch in bitch—and so can you, Girlfriend. But the bottom line is, Why? There's no need for it. You can get more flies with honey than you can with vinegar. And this does not have to cause numerous changes on your part.

Yeah, I know . . . your family, your friends, your lover (or lovers, depending on your need for variety), and your employers or employees can kick your butt and dog you out. But what really counts is after it's all said and done, did you do the best you could do? Did you try everything you could try? If you can answer yes to these two questions, then you can go to sleep peacefully because you ain't got nothin' else to worry about, baby.

Everybody always asks me, "Mother Love, what makes you tick? What sets you apart from everybody else?"

I don't know. I have no clue. My needs, wants, and desires are no different from anybody else's. In fact, if you knew half the stuff I've been through you might put this book down right now. But I can tell you this: Mother Love is a kick-butt, no-holds-barred, take-no-crap-from-nobody kind of Girlfriend.

I'm gonna love you honestly and tell you the truth straight up, which you may not like. But hey, so many things in life you ain't gonna like. At least you're gonna hear it from someone who doesn't lie, someone who will tell you the truth when others won't, someone who won't stand there and grin in your face and then laugh behind your back at your misfortune—or whatever the situation is.

Mother Love is reality, truth, humor, and laughter. She talks about all the things you Girlfriends think and feel but just don't have the nerve to say. Being Mother Love is my innate gift from God, from a divine being who touched me with the ability to touch and teach other people with laughter. I don't slap God in the face with it. I appreciate it and want to share it with you, Girlfriend.

Sometimes I have to stand back and take stock of who

I am, where I'm going, and what lessons I still need to learn. Yeah, Girlfriend, there are lessons to be learned. Lessons that you have to learn and that you will teach your children. Lessons based on years of wisdom that will show you how to create a life of love.

My wisdom is my mother's wisdom and her mother's wisdom. And you can throw in a few aunts and cousins with all the other wisdom handed down from generation to generation.

My auntie and my mother used to have the most amazing conversations, buzzing back and forth like a couple of bees. I would sit in front of them with my mouth open, enthralled, and mother always used to say, "Well, do you want me to get a dang tape recorder so you don't miss nothing?"

I would say, "Yeah! Could you? Please? Because I know I'm going to miss something."

I wanted to be in on their conversations because they were so much fun. They were hilarious. So many bits and pieces of wisdom. As they spoke they were developing the woman I was becoming.

The wisdom never ends. It becomes fine-tuned as we learn from our mistakes, make the necessary corrections, and go back into the world, whether it be personal or professional. Go out and kick big-time butt—and then take names!

This is my roots, where I came from: the Cleveland projects

Who else? My mother!

Mother love ©

CHAPTER ONE

This ain't no party—so take notes.
—My Husband

❤ ❤ ❤

If I'd had my druthers I'd have been born a queen somewhere, runnin' the show. I wouldn't have been born no
poor-ass Girlfriend from the Cleveland projects—which is
a very nice way of saying "the ghetto"—but that's the way
it was.

In my family there were six kids. And we always had
somebody extra living with us. Some stray. My mother
was always taking in strays. Some people take in stray dogs
and cats; well, my mother was always taking in stray families.

She'd say, "Well, you know, babies, you've gotta always help someone less fortunate than you."

And I would say, "Ma! Who is less fortunate than us?
We live in the projects. We poor people in the ghetto,
okay? Work with me here, baby—wake up, Ma!"

My mother: "No, there are people who are less fortunate than you."

And I'm thinking, Well, these people must be dead by now—what is she talking about?

Even though we lived in the projects, and we knew we were poor, my mother never let us believe that we were poor. She worked all the time and because of this she felt like she wasn't giving us enough. What she couldn't give us in time she made up for with money and food.

Give us a reason and we celebrated when I was growing up! Pork chops, homemade biscuits, fresh syrup. We celebrated Sunday, we celebrated Tuesday; my mother could "hit the number," somebody could get a job or have a baby. We celebrated life with food.

But of all the things my mother gave me when I was growing up, the thirst for knowledge was her greatest gift. She'd have us reading newspapers, magazines, cereal boxes, the labels on cans, and, of course, the Bible. My mother was very well educated and would say, "Every time you read, you learn—and this will color every part of your life. This will help you find your purpose in life. With purpose comes pride. And with pride comes a healthy self-love."

WHAT'S HOLDING YOU BACK, GIRLFRIEND?

When my mother encouraged us to read, learn, find our purpose, have a sense of pride, and develop a healthy dose of self-love, her intention was not to prepare us for love and marriage. In fact, my mother was a serious male basher. She was angry because my father had died when she was thirty and left her with six children.

For as wise as my mother was, she just didn't get it when it came to men. This was one topic we never agreed on. Yeah, my mother was hard on men. And it was her anger that held her back from having a second husband. I watched really nice, intelligent, vibrant men love my mother and I watched her chew them up and spit them out between her teeth.

My mother's daily litany was that men were users, no good, and were just gonna leave you; that they would just find you, snatch your panties, and forget you. She was pretty raw in her description of all of this and had us terrified for a long time.

As I grew up, I realized my mother's philosophy about men was ridiculous. Why? Because I had always liked boys. And I really loved men!

But beneath all the male-bashing, I knew my mother was right about two things: the importance of finding our purpose and the necessity of developing our self-love. And this was not because my sisters and I were doomed to spend our lives without men. A sense of purpose and developing self-love could only improve all of our relationships— especially with men.

3

You want love in your life?

Then know your purpose.

Let me illustrate:

Girlfriend: "You know, Mother Love, I can't find a man. I want one to catch the rats, buy me new clothes, pay off my car, be built like Mr. Universe, have a million-dollar smile, have an endless supply of money, be the world's greatest lover straight out of a fashion magazine, and one who will love my mother and love my dog."

Me: "Okay, baby, now what are you willing to
do for him?"

Girlfriend: "Well, I don't know 'cause I had
somebody break my heart and I ain't
gonna do all that crap for no man no
more because I'm sick and tired of this!"

Me: "Excuse me, but that's why you don't have
a man."

And then I ask you, "What is it that you
want? What is it that you want for you,
independent from a man? Shoot, forget
about the man. Where do you see
yourself in three years, five years, ten
years and so on?"

Girlfriend (your voice starts losing its edge):
"You know, Mother Love, I don't know
what I want. . . ."

And that's when I have to tell you, "Well, this is the first
thing you better figure out, Girlfriend, because you can't
expect some man who cannot mind-read (especially some
man with a brain like a pea) to come into your life and
make you happy when you tell him, 'I want you to love me
and give me everything that I need—but I don't know what
it is that I need, so I can't tell you what I need, so just
guess!' "

Now think of the poor man, scratchin' his head
(doesn't matter which head). "I love you but you're kinda
crazy. You don't know what you want. You're sending
me through these emotional tailspins—heck, if you would
just tell me what you want maybe I could give it to
you."

Oh Lord, and then you start again: "You don't
    love me! You don't understand me! Why
    are you treating me this way?"
Boyfriend: "Well, can we sit down and talk
    and—"
You: "No, I don't wanna talk!"

And by this time Boyfriend doesn't want to talk either. Is
it any wonder?
    You don't know what to talk about.
    You don't know what you want.
    You don't know what you've got.
    You don't know who you are.
    All because you haven't figured out what your pur-
pose is.

    You've got to know all of these things, especially your
purpose, before you begin a relationship so that you know
what you're bringing to the table. The whole point of a
relationship goes like this: "I got that over here and you've
got this over there. Now we gonna put everything that
we've got as a couple on the table and we're just gonna be
pigs! We can live *phat*!"
    My purpose?
    Before I was Mother Love I was "Sister Love," but
I didn't know it. When people got sick in the projects
my mother would send me to them to entertain. When
someone would die they would call the minister, the
morgue, and me. I'd ask Mother, "Aw, Ma, why do I gotta go?"

    My mother: "Well, baby, you're gonna make
      them laugh. You're gonna make them feel

5

better. And it won't seem like such a bad thing. You just go in there and be your usual charming self and everything will be okay."

I was always thinking: usual, charming—what is she talking about? This is crap only your mother would tell you.

But by the time I was fifteen I began to understand that I could make people laugh, especially when they were feeling sick, tired, and down in the dumps. This gave me a purpose. But it was my choice to develop it. Make it something special. Become Mother Love.

So, Girlfriend, it is your personal responsibility to find out who you are and where you fit in—your purpose. And finding it is only the beginning. You have to take it, work it, and make it yours. This responsibility doesn't fall on your parents, lovers, husband, children, or co-workers, and yet you use them as an excuse for not being the best that you can be.

❤   ❤   ❤

"My mama didn't love me."

"My papa was never home."

"My brother always embarrassed me in front of my friends."

"My boss is always taking credit for my work."

When I hear these tired, old, rerun excuses I really have to wonder. Don't you think it's time to let this old stuff go? And if not, do you mean to tell me that you allow people to have such jurisdiction over your life that you can't move forward?

Girlfriend, you don't allow anyone to have that kind of control over your life. If you do, then they ought to be runnin' the show, they ought to be telling you what to do, and they ought to be talkin' about you like you're a dog. Woof!

Dang!

Girlfriend!

Where's your self-love?

When someone attacks me I tell 'em, "Knock yourself out! Shoot your best shot! Come on with it, baby, I'm here with you—'cause when I get a chance I'm gonna chew your big butt up and spit it out and leave it for Tuesday's trash!"

What about you? Nothing you do, say, or feel should come from a lack of self-love, optimism, or faith. You lose these and you are shot to hell, taking everyone around with you!

♥

7

♥

MY COMFORT ZONE

What feels good to you?

Who are you?

What are the boundaries that make up your comfort zone?

Personally, I can't settle for anything unless it feels right. And of course the moment I start fighting back, the moment I realize that I don't have to take the crap that's being dished out, people start talking, "Oh see, now she's acting like a bitch—oh, yeah—who does she think she is? I thought she was real nice and sweet and we could just run over her!"

Excuse me?

Let's not mistake kindness for weakness.

I'm very silly but I'm not stupid.

I believe I'm a good team player.

I have strong leadership skills.

I am genius personified!

I think I have a great sense of humor.

I think I'm a loving, giving person.

These are all the good things about me, Mother Love
. . . *but*

I ain't all hearts and flowers!

I can put the itch in bitch.

You would rather run through hell in gasoline drawers than fool with me!

I'm tough.

I don't like bullshit people.

Especially that kissy-kissy bullshit-bullshit.

I don't like bullshit run up under me.

And I don't like bullshit people trying to put bullshit under me and giving attitude because I know it's bullshit coming from bullshit people!

This is the way I am.

That's the way I'm gonna be.

Period.

Different attitudes work for different people. This is what works for me, and has especially worked for me when it comes to dealing with me. I say if bullshit is your game, take it somewhere else, baby!

STEPPING INTO WHO YOU ARE

You're worried that if you're not a size six you won't get a good man?

You're gettin' older—what man would want to take a second look?

What kind of man is going to fall for a woman with very short legs like yours?

That big butt is still sagging here and there—even

after all those hours at the gym. Do you dare wear those spandex pants?

The list of these Girlfriend questions could be endless, because no matter how physically perfect any of us are there's always somethin' for us to pick at. I'm not saying that we shouldn't try to improve, but let's not get ridiculous. Some things will never change.

I've got one hip that's larger than the other because of a car accident that happened when I was seventeen. Now if you think that I'm going to let some bonehead doctor whittle away at my big hip so that I have a matched set, you're crazy.

And then there are my "toe dots."

God didn't give me toenails. God gave me these toe dots, which my manicurist sees to be a means for her artistic expression: "Painting your toenails is like painting rice . . . very delicate . . . very pretty."

Never be ashamed of who you are, what you are, what you've got to strut, or how old you are. You have to love yourself no matter where you are in your life: too short, too tall, too big, too small, too common, *too anything*—toe dots and all!

In order to be ready for love, you've got to get yourself together. You have to love you physically. This means that from your head to your toes you have to accept the good with the bad and the ugly:

Stop!

Stand back!

Check yourself out!

Ask yourself, Why do I love myself and why do I hate myself?

I have seen me, Mother Love, stark naked in a full-length mirror with no makeup, no nail polish, no hairdo—

no fancy nothin'! After I pick myself up off the floor, laughing hysterically, I say, "I'm all right! I'm all right! I'm okay with me."

I'm okay with my big droopy titties, my big fat belly, and my little short toes with their toe dots. . . . I'm okay anyhow!

Girlfriend, I'm so far from perfect, but I'm all right 'cause I can look at that chick in the mirror and when I look at her I like her. She smiles back at me and we're all right! Now we're going to put on some panties and a good bra, and we're gonna get the day started.

Now, if I didn't like me I'd be a bitter, jealous, jaded, don't-wanna-see-anybody-else's-happiness kind of chick! When you can't go eye-to-eye with yourself and be satisfied, you don't even want to think of anybody else being happy. I call it "scratchin'."

You start "scratchin'" at other people with your "Ooh-ooh, I'm gonna hate you for whatever reason. I don't want you to have that"—scratch away, scratch away! And every time you scratch at another person, you're scratching away at yourself. But so many of you Girlfriends don't get this.

You've got to focus on only you until you're all right with yourself. This is where the healing begins. If you start the healing with yourself, everything else will fall into place. We've got to stop thinking things like "She would be fine if she lost eighty-five pounds . . ." about ourselves and others.

Now, you all don't really want to see Mother Love eighty-five pounds thinner because I'm liable to become one of those *Playboy* chicks runnin' around with my titties flappin'—because I'm a big exhibitionist anyway! And I would not have on any clothes except for those little string panties—you know, the kind that hide up your butt. So this is a good thing for me (and probably my neighbors) that I've got those extra eighty-five pounds.

Even if I did lose all this weight and all the rest of the people in the country lost the weight that they're hassled about, Hershey's, Sara Lee, and NordicTrack would go out of business in six months. Shoot, I just wouldn't be able to sleep at night knowing I'd put so many people in the un-employment line! I'd rather eat big muffins, keep my pounds in place, and know that I'm helping the economy. And besides all of this, how could I continue to be a spokesperson for a full-figure line of clothing as a size eight? Mother Love is here to give these little skinny one-bone chicks a run for their money!

Yeah! Fat and happy—but I didn't say sloppy.

I wanna clean up the fat, sloppy women because they're giving us a bad name. You know who they are—you've seen 'em. The kind you want to take, with their sloppy, big butts, and lock away in a shed somewhere.

Call the fashion police to arrest them! The charge? Wearing those ugly, black, fuzz-ball-covered polyester pants that are stuck up so far (grotta so deep) that it's a wonder those women aren't cut in half. And then they've got a bra on that they know is two cup sizes too small, making them look like they've got six tits.

I have to tell them, "Get a bigger bra, baby. It's not that hard to do—why you wanna look like you've got six tits? C'mon, work with me, baby."

I come from a big family, both in number and girth, and I'm the smallest one in the family. I never grew up with that ridiculous cliché, "You have such a pretty face, *but* if only you . . ." Girlfriend, you know the rest.

My mother would say, "Honey, you're big? Decorate it! Think of yourself as a big house. Put some pictures on the wall—don't be afraid to deck yourself out!"

YOUR SPIRITUAL HOME

Girlfriend, how are you going to have a good relationship with anyone if you don't have a good one with yourself first? And we all need a little help, especially when we're feeling really low and dogged out about ourselves. Girlfriend, take the time to find yourself a place of grace; a special place where you connect with "God," whatever you conceive "God" to be. Personally, I don't trust anyone who doesn't believe in some kind of God and doesn't have sex!

My brothers and sisters and I were introduced to God as our mother knew God. We weren't allowed just to be pew warmers. This meant church services, Sunday school, tithing, and participation in the choir. The minister and church leaders knew us by name. And Sister Rivers knew my name just a little too well! Yeah, I was always cuttin' up when it was time to be silent.

And you could never, in the presence of my mother, talk about fat people, ugly people, or handicapped people. There was no "Oh look! Look at that man with the hump in his back" ever allowed to be spoken. If we said anything, we would have to stop where we were, pray right then and there, saying "Oh, look at that man with the hump in his back. . . . Thank you, Lord, that I don't have a hump in my back. Please, dear Lord Jesus, pray for this man with the hump in his back that his life is not too complicated." And the finale: "There but for the grace of God go I."

The littler kids would ask, "What does that mean? What's she talkin' about?" When we got home one of us

12

would have to go get the Bible and we'd all have to sit down and have a Bible lesson.

While my mother had introduced us as children to God as she knew God, as we grew up she told us, "My God ain't your God. Once you're old enough to make your decision as to who your God is going to be, be committed and convicted to him or her or whatever, but know, beyond a shadow of a doubt, that there is a greater being than you because you're just a little Biscuit Head, stupid, peon.

"You can't make a tree.

"You can't make a blade of grass.

"You can't make the wind blow.

"Focus on what you can do instead of what you can't do.

"You can make a heart happy.

"You can make yourself glad.

"You can have great kids.

"You can be a good friend.

"You can be a loving person.

"These are the choices you have. Try to make the right decisions."

At moments like this, my mother seemed to have the ability to stop time. As often as she and I would go toe-to-toe, how could I not love her for the wisdom she shared—of course when *she* chose to. Now, as a grown woman, when I think of my mother, I glory in her spunk!

Today, if I'm not in church and I find I need a meeting with my maker I sit on the floor by my bed with my Bible and pray. Or I'll sit on the floor of my shower and just let the water run over me for as long as it takes for me to feel better. Sometimes it seems that the whole shower lights up. When I emerge my husband will say, "Oh, my! That shower of yours was certainly invigorating."

13

Even if you don't see God as a divine entity, you have to have something to hold on to. Maybe your God is a sofa, so you hold on to that pink sofa during those bad times. Although I must warn you that the sofa will wear out, but God's unchanging hand won't.

The point, Girlfriend, is that spirituality is one of the best resources you have to make yourself feel okay. We all need a place in our hearts, in our minds, and even in our bodies where we can go and have an honest one-on-one with ourselves, a place to plug into so that we can truly connect with a higher being and feel whole again.

♥ HERE'S THE HORSE—WHAT HAPPENED
14 TO THE PRINCE?
♥

You're ready. You really want to meet the man you can spend the rest of your life with—yesssss, Mr. Wonderful! *But:*

> Girlfriend: "I'd never date a guy who already
> has kids."
> Me: "Well, then, that ruins your chances with a
> large percentage of the male population."

Seriously, what happens if the guy you love, the guy you are convinced is your soul mate, has told you about everything *but* his children? And then one evening he says he has something very special to tell you. You hold your breath as he reaches into his pocket for what could be an engagement ring, but instead he pulls out his wallet. As he opens his wallet the plastic flaps of photos come tumbling out.

Not a diamond. (See, you jumped the gun.)

A wallet with plastic photo flaps.

There are at least five flaps. Oh Lord, does this mean five children?

Whether it's one child or five children, are you not gonna love this man because of this child or these children? Is this engraved in stone?

I know Girlfriends who will not date men who make less than $50,000 a year. But what happens if you meet a garbageman and he's making $28,000 a year and he is a good man, a good provider, and loves you unconditionally?

What most of us don't understand about love and being in a relationship is that *true love really is unconditional.* You don't tell somebody, "Oh I love you, *but . . .*" It should be, "I love you *and . . .*" To me this is the test of real love: it doesn't have "but"s, only "and"s.

You ain't never gonna find yourself a lifelong partner until all of your "but"s become "and"s.

Period.

Confidence draws men like flies to honey.

Ain't no skinny chick dyin' to get out of me!

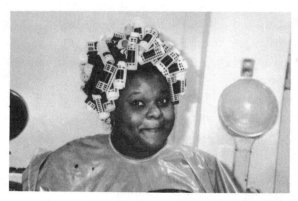

Make yourself pretty and keep yourself clean enough to eat off at all times, Girlfriend!

CHAPTER TWO

Don't meet a man with your panties in your purse!
—Mother Love

❤   ❤   ❤

*S*omeone should have told my auntie about keepin' on her panties when she and Uncle went out drinking. My auntie could cuss and tell people off like nobody's business! She'd pull off her panties and start: "You kiss my ass, you sorry son of a biscuit eater—splobb you and the horse you rode in on!"

Uncle was no help. In fact he would get so drunk that with one punch Auntie could knock him out!

Now, if Auntie was lookin' for a new man to replace Uncle, I don't think that pulling her panties off, lifting her dress, and parting her cheeks in front of men she did not know was a good way to get acquainted.

Mama would get a phone call, and I would go with her to the bar, get Auntie, put her panties back on her, and bring her and Uncle home. In all fairness I have to say that when they were sober, my auntie and uncle were the nicest people you could imagine.

My auntie and her panty antics taught me at an early age that you don't meet men with your panties in your purse. You may carry an extra pair of panties in your purse with an extra pair of panty hose, but, Girlfriend, without some nice clean panties pulled up around your fanny you aren't complete. Wearing panties gives you a nice feeling that you're really dressed and ready to take on what the world has to offer in the way of men.

DUNDERHEADS I HAVE KNOWN AND HOPE NEVER TO MEET AGAIN

19

Before you worry about meeting a new man, you may want to revisit some of your experiences with the previous dunderheads you've known and "loved." Why repeat your mistakes from the past? Yeah, I've been with some strange guys too. Girlfriend, you know what I mean.

I was fifteen when I fell for this big guy with a nice beard. He was no boy—he was a nineteen- or twenty-year-old man! He was so cute and sweet. He bought me clothes, a coat, jewelry, came over for Christmas, had a black convertible, and dressed real nice, neat, and clean.

On my birthday and Christmas he loaded me up with presents. Oh, he just loved my dirty underwear! My head got so big and my brothers and sisters are going, "Ooooooooooh, Mama! You should see all the stuff Boyfriend got for Sister. Oooooooh!"

Mama took me upstairs and told me, "Now, you ain't gonna like this, but you have to give it all back. . . ."

Me: "Uh-uh! No, Mama, noooooo! I don't
  wanna."

Mama: "Now, you have to give all this stuff
   back because you're only fifteen years old.
   That's a grown man down there and he is
   going to want something for all those
   presents."

Me: "Want? What he gonna want? I can't give
  it to him? I'll give it to him . . . whatever
  it is. He can't want too much."

Mama: "He's gonna want something."

Me: "No, he ain't gonna want something. He's
  not like that. He's a very nice man. . . ."

♥

20

♥

I was right. He didn't want nothing, then.

By spring he was still showering me with presents and
gifts, would pay for me to get my hair done and kept my
wardrobe updated. One night he took me out to a special
barbecue restaurant and behind it was a hotel.

After filling me with great ribs and fries, he slides over
to my side of the car real fast.

"What are we doin' here now? Are you buying me
seconds?" I had forgotten about my mother's warning because so much time had passed.

Bearded Boyfriend said, "I want some sex from you."

I said, "You have sex—you're a man and I'm a woman."

"This is not funny. I have been taking really good care
of you and I think it's time for you to give me SEX!"

I freaked out as Bearded Boyfriend tried to get his
very big arms around me. I kicked his windshield in and
kicked the side window out and I screamed and screamed
like nothin' he'd heard before. Thank the Lord I had my
panties on!

He panicked and started screaming back, "No! Okay! I'm sorry! I'm sorry! Just calm down! It's okay, it's okay!"

"No! Take me home! Take me home!" As soon as we got to the front of the house I jumped out of the car and never saw that man again. (But, I did keep the presents!)

❤   ❤   ❤

I had one dunderhead boyfriend who looked like my father. I was fascinated by this, and I was sure my mother would be thrilled because my father had been the only man who could stop her in her tracks.

My mother came down the stairs and saw Boyfriend with my father's same fair coloring and his same build. Oh yeah, she saw him, and she looked him up and down and then she said, "You're just doin' this stuff out of spite! Why? Why? Why does this one have to look like your daddy?"

> Me: "Well, he must be lookin' pretty wierd if
>   he looks like your dead husband, because
>   your husband has been dead for a number
>   of years. Ma, he don't look that bad."
> Mother: "Get out of my damn face!"

I dated this guy for about a month. And yes, I dated him because he did look like my daddy. I probably had something like an "Electra complex."

Anyway, he came over to my house one night and sat down. When he saw the tray of crackers on the table he said, "Ooooooh, I didn't know you had this much class."

> Me: "What do you mean when you say I have
>   'this much class'?"

He: "I never been to no girl's house where they
be eatin' cheese and cheevy crackers."

Me: "What the hell is a cheevy? What's a
cheevy?"

He: "Look right here—the box says cheese and
cheevy crackers."

Girlfriend, I'm thinking that there's no way that we can go
out, that this isn't going to work. I said, "I have a headache.
I will see you later. You have to go."

When he left I screamed, "Ma! Ma! Come here! Do
you know what these are?"

"What?"

"These are cheese and cheevy crackers."

We both laughed and agreed that this dunderhead
had to be the biggest fool God put on this green earth.
The "cheese and cheevy crackers" were actually cheese and
chive crackers. Mother turned to me and said, "You don't
date a guy that looks like your dead daddy. And you don't
date a guy who can take a one-syllable word and turn it
into two syllables!"

It's a good idea to stay away from anyone that igno-
rant—and I don't care who they look like. But ever since
then I have called chives "cheevies." I'll be in a restaurant
and ask for just a baked potato and cheevies. And people
get it. Dang!

GET THE RIFFRAFF OUT OF YOUR LIFE

I get a call from a Girlfriend who has a twenty-one-year-
old daughter. She has raised her daughter as a single parent
because the guy that got her pregnant is violent and dom-

22

ineering. As we are talking I think my ears are on fire: she's talking about this same guy she was with twenty-one years ago and how she still wants to be in love with him!

> Me: "Your daughter is grown and she must be
> the only one of you with a brain in her
> head!"

All Girlfriend wants to do is to hold on to this guy and the passion they had in the past. I guess they did make passionate love when they were eighteen or nineteen, but who didn't at that age?

And with this boyfriend there was a hitch. Either before or after they made love he'd beat her and blacken her eyes—and then he'd make love to her again! He was beating her all the time and he warned her to stay away from me because I was telling her how inappropriate his behavior was. He was a heavy drinker, and besides her, he was havin' every chick he could lay his hands on. He wore jeans and a white T-shirt with his cigarettes rolled up in his sleeves like James Dean. Everybody thought he was so tough and so macho. But I thought he was just a chump.

All I could ever say to him was "How can you even think of callin' yourself a man when you're beatin' up women?" Now, he would beat up men, too, so he wasn't just a woman abuser. But him punching women was the worst.

Girlfriend would allow herself to be his punching bag, and I would ask her, "How can you let him beat on you that way?"

She would say—*and women fall for this all the time*—"But he says he loves me."

23

Me: "You can't love something you beat on a
regular basis. He ain't payin' your rent or
doin' nothin' for you but blackening your
eyes, and we're runnin' to the store
buying steaks to put on your face!"

Girlfriends, everywhere, get away from *him* no matter
how much he tells you he loves you and how sorry he is.
You cannot believe anything some man says while he's
knockin' on you. You should feel better about yourself than
even to think about allowin' someone to be punchin' on
you and bashin' your face in. This ain't no man—this is
"riffraff"!

24

Oh, Riffraff will tell you, "Who's gonna want you with
three babies? I can kick your butt anytime I feel like it.
Nobody is gonna want ugly old you with three babies!"

I've had too many Girlfriends in this situation who I
had to help. They've come to me terrified, babies under
their arms, and I've hidden them and their children in my
house. Some learn and others go right back for more when
their cuts and bruises heal.

If you allow your butt to get kicked all the time you're
just abandoning yourself. For as much as you've been kicked, you gotta kick the "riffraff" out of your life.

If Girlfriend says, "Well, he just don't know what to
do without me," I gotta tell her, "Every time you go in the
hospital he knows what to do without you, so don't you be
tellin' me how everything goes to pot when you're gone.
Girlfriend, you're just fallin' into that same old crap."

And emotional abuse can be just as bad. But it takes
on a different form. No, the nasty remarks and put-downs
will not blacken your eyes, but they sure can bruise your

self-esteem. Riffraff will do everything in his power to wear you down and dog you out just with his words:

> Riffraff: "Oh, so you think you're going to meet your girlfriend for lunch? What about the money it costs? You're just a selfish bitch who don't give a damn! You look like hell in those pants! Just look at your ass, stickin' out all funny. And what is it with those earrings—God, you're a sight!"
>
> Or: "I told you I wanted a steak tonight—not a hamburger! What's wrong with you? Is there any life in that pea brain of yours? Forget about dinner—I'm going out to have a beer. Maybe I'll score! Anything is better than you!"
>
> Or: "Your mother called again. Don't you dare call her back—all she wants to do is bitch and moan about her arthritis! I ain't payin' for no long-distance calls to your sorry excuse for a mother. And you're as pathetic as she is!"

No "riffraff" should have any woman hook, line, and sinker! Break the pattern and set yourself free! But know that it's not just going to get better. Girlfriend, you're gonna have to fight. Rant, rave, and scream, and *fight back.* Don't be walking on eggshells. Get a restraining order from the police and contact women's shelters and other resources for help if you're caught up with some "riffraff" in an abusive situation.

DON'T BE A SKAINTCH

No more dunderheads.

Put the "riffraff" behind bars where they belong and let's get down to the serious business of meeting new men.

Okay?

Time for panty chat again:

You don't meet a man with your panties in your purse.

Don't laugh. I'm serious about this. Your panties should be on because *anybody* will like you with your panties off.

Keep your bloomers on your butt!

I know so many "skaintchy" women. They're the women wearing scandalous clothes, no panties under their short miniskirts as they strut their stuff with their high heels on, showing off their football-player legs. When they bend over you can read their name, address, and telephone number across their big behinds! Shoot, you can pick up any kind of man like that because you're just givin' it away.

A skaintch has probably got a baby or two at home, but she doesn't want to give them up. She just wants to be a skaintch! She wants to be all over the men. She's the kind of woman who would meet a man with her panties in her purse. I don't want any of you Girlfriends to be that type of woman because a skaintch smells of D-E-S-P-E-R-A-T-I-O-N!

Bein' a skaintch is no way to be if you're lookin' for your lifelong partner! You can look ravishing and sexy, tastefully, without looking desperate.

We've all been taught by the "fashion experts" that the trick is to dress proportionally to your body size and shape. I've seen some really big Girlfriends who look great in a pantsuit because they've got no rolls of fat and their bodies are in proportion to fit their big size. Now you put this same pantsuit on a short little squat woman and she be lookin' like a fool!

Don't be a skaintch and don't be a fashion fool. Find what looks good on you. Find your fashion sense: go to all the stores, try on combinations and different styles. Take the time. Personally, I'm a big accessory nut and I love colors. I also like prints and patterns.

And if you plan on living a long time, and don't want to spend every penny you have on clothes but need to diet, aim for a reasonable size and stay there. It's hard to stay a size ten when your starving body is screaming size fourteen! I know because there ain't no skinny chick dyin' to get out of me.

I've got Girlfriends with three to five different sizes of clothing jammed into their closets. Forget about planning an evening out meeting new men—so many girlfriends never leave their houses because "what to wear" is holding them hostage.

KEEP YOURSELF CLEAN ENOUGH TO EAT OFF OF AT ALL TIMES

In taking pride in yourself, whether you're getting ready to meet a new man or just for the sake of your own self-esteem, personal hygiene is number one on the list. I don't care if you're a size two or a size fifty-two, make sure that you are *clean*. Your skin, your hair—everything, everywhere.

Dirty hair has the worst smell in the world. Don't use hot rollers, curling irons, or any kind of heat—you'll just end up smelling like a dead squirrel. And there is no such thing as "a natural smell." This is just a polite way of saying, "You stink!"

We naturally don't smell good at all. Armpits stink, groins stink, mouths stink, your hair can stink—that's why we have soap, deodorant, toilet paper, and toothpaste. This probably sounds crazy to many of you because good hy giene is presumed more than it's practiced. But, Girlfriend, check it out:

> You gotta wipe your butt,
> Brush your teeth,
> Comb your hair,
> And wash those feet!

Consistently good hygiene habits are a must. Everywhere for anywhere, keep yourself clean enough to eat off of at all times. Wash, even if you must take a PTA bath—pits, tits & ass bath!

While you don't meet a man with your panties in your purse, you never know when you might have to put your panties in your purse. Ya just never know when that moment might come, so ya gotta be kissing soft and spring fresh!

Beyond staying spit-shine clean:

Go to the dentist and keep your gums and teeth healthy. A dazzling smile shows confidence. Yeah, use that floss and mouthwash that leaves your teeth and gums plaque-free.

And whether they're long or short, take care of your nails. Your hands are usually the first part of you to touch another person. I used to be a chronic nail-biter, but nobody ever knew because I always wore fake fingernails. I carried glue wherever I went so that if one popped off or fell in a drink, I could just glue that bad boy back on. When I arrived in L.A. six years ago, the one thing I was determined to do for myself was get acrylic nails. Eventually, I kicked my nail-biting habit and was able to grow my own nails. I take great pride in this because I now have really pretty hands.

Bad hair? Get yourself a hair weave, baby. Personally, I have come to accept the fact that the hair that grows out of my head, so fine, limp, and fragile, is for putting a "wig-hat" on with a bobby pin (I've got about fifteen "wig-hats" and I call them my other Girlfriends) or for making sure a track can be sewn in to attach a hair weave to.

What else?

Know your assets and play them up for all their worth—legs, ankles, waist, behind, bustline—just don't go gettin' skaintchy about it. Each and every one of us has at least two to three great attributes we can work with.

And stuff your lingerie drawer with panties that flatter your butt, hips, and thighs: bikini cut, thigh-high cut, or just good old satin drawers. Go for it, Girlfriend!

One of my Girlfriends used to spend whatever was left over of her paycheck, after she paid the bills, to buy sexy lingerie. She's got beautiful long legs, but she's got a belly. One day she called me, fretting over what to wear because Boyfriend was comin' over and she didn't have anything new.

> Girlfriend: "Mother Love—help! Boyfriend is on his way over for the night and he's seen everything I have."
> Me: "Do you have clean panties?"
> Girlfriend: "Yes."
> Me: "Do you have thigh-high cut panties to show off them pretty long legs?"
> Girlfriend: "Well, yeah."

Me: "Now get yourself one of your over-
     sized T-shirts with a logo on it and cut
     that logo out so that he's seeing cleavage
     for days! And belly problem is solved
     too!"

LOOKING GOOD NO MATTER WHAT

Next to cleanliness, begin every day as if it is the most
important day of your life. I don't care if the only living
thing you're planning on seeing is your dog or cat, from
the moment you wake up, prepare! Fix your hair and get
your makeup on (in my case I've gotta put both on!) so that
you're ready for anything or anyone the day may bring.
Dressed up or casual, you should always look your best—
or close to it—even if your only planned activity is a trip
to the grocery store!

THE RENDEZVOUS

Ready to meet some of them?
    Check out some of these "everyday places":
    The grocery store is an excellent place to meet men
because you're doing what I consider to be a "wifin'" thing.
And all men, regardless of anything else women might do,
like women who still do "wifin'" things.
    Regardless of the current trend, you can't expect to
get a man, let alone keep one, without some "wifin' skills."
I know this makes many of you think, "Oh God!" But since
prehistoric times woman have tended to the domestic needs
of man.
    Now don't pull attitude, Girlfriend. This is just some-

thing you're going to have to do at least a little of. I'm not saying that you should fire the housekeeper, but why don't you call up your mother and ask her about wifing? She probably has done it and still does do it, and so can you! What it's really about is caring for someone so that you can allow yourself to be cared *for!*

Let's go, Girlfriend!

Go armed with your coupons and act like you know exactly what you're doing, even if you don't know a honeydew from a cantaloupe. I've had more guys stop and ask me how to cook a chicken, how to cook pork chops besides frying them, what's a kiwi, and on and on.

If you know next to nothin' about cooking, get yourself a cookbook and study it just so you know about the different foods and how to shop. And remember, regardless of how fat-conscious we've all become, men still love a good meal of meat and potatoes.

When you're in the meat department, touch the rump roasts with your pretty manicured hands, seductively pick up a package of ground round, and inspect those chickens like you're getting ready to prepare a meal for a king. Men will watch you and ask you how you can tell a good chicken from a bad chicken. Girlfriend, a good chicken has a rich yellow color and a bad one looks white. And of course you should always pick a fresh chicken over a frozen one. A few more quick tips you can share with him in the grocery store:

- Check for the date on the packages and double-check the freshness.

- Watch for sales.

♥
31
♥

- Get a good cut of meat—and tell him to watch for the "marble" in meat (instead of using the word *fat*).

- Fresh fish does not smell fishy.

- Generic products can be just as good as brand names.

Trust me, Girlfriend, he'll be impressed that not only do you look good enough to eat, but you know how to cook so that you both can eat!

♥   ♥   ♥   ♥

32   Another good spot to impress men with your "wifin' " skills is
♥   the Laundromat. Most men are loaded down with weeks of dirty laundry when they arrive. They're confused by their numerous unpaired socks, embarrassed about their dirty drawers, and frustrated with their laundry in general. But there you are, armed with detergent, bleach, and fabric softener.

Let him watch you gently fold your delicate lingerie, your bras and panties, clean, not dirty. If they are dirty, make sure that if you drop them on the floor, and he steps on them, they aren't so funky they crack!

♥   ♥   ♥

And then there's the gas station where any man will be more than happy to help you out if you look like you're having trouble pumping your own gas. Yeah, I know most of you Girlfriends can change your own oil and fix a flat, but let the gas station remain their territory. Okay?

Handsome stranger: "Can I pump that for you? Want me to fill you up?"
Me: "Oooooh, yeah . . ."

Now, I can talk like that because I'm married. Just because I'm full doesn't mean I can't look at the menu. Even as a married woman I still flirt with men because I want to make sure I haven't lost my skills. Like any art, it must be practiced or it will be lost!

💜　💜　💜

Start going to church, synagogue, temple, or whatever. Just think: it's one of the few places where you can meet with your maker and meet a man.

When you go to church, be looking like a church-going woman. This means no eye-popping cleavage or tight-fitting anything. Nothing like a nice church dress where you're all covered up, looking kind of pure and virginal . . . but wear some really sexy perfume.

I wear my church clothes at home sometimes because it just makes my husband—and I don't know why—go beserk!

If you like kids, on weekends try the park, where single dads usually hang out with their kids. Also keep yourself community- and civic-minded; good people in general care about the well-being of the community they live in.

And do something that you wouldn't normally do.

Girlfriend says, "I'd like to meet a nice guy and have kids—or even meet a guy who already has kids."

I say, "Become a Big Sister—get involved with a program that gives you a one-on-one relationship with a child. Forget about the guy for now."

Girlfriend: "I ain't doing that!"
Me: "See, that's your problem. You've got to be willing to be with someone who needs you unconditionally. See if you can deal

💜

33

💜

with it. The experience will certainly take
a lot of the crap out of you and make it
very real. And in the process you'll find
out about the stuff you're made of, if you
would make a good mommy and a good
wife."

♥   ♥   ♥

Regardless of where you are, the store, the gas station,
Laundromat, church, always make it seem like you've already got a man—in fact make it seem like you've got
two!

How do you do this when the opposite is true?

Keep yourself fixed up, always wear a smile on your
face, and act very busy, like you've got lots of places to go,
things to do, and you're not even sure which boyfriend
you'll be seeing tonight!

Bottom line? Don't ever look desperate because men
can smell desperation at forty paces—and the first thing
they start thinkin' is "skaintch."

So just do your life, take pride in your appearance,
keep your panties on, wear a smile on your face, and watch
what happens. It can really be that simple!

MAKING YOUR APPROACH

What's the biggest attraction women can have for men
across the board? Confidence. When a man can see that a
woman is confident—not arrogant, but confident—in herself that's what will attract him. An arrogant woman takes
pride in herself, but assumes every man will kiss her feet.
A confident woman takes pride in herself, but assumes nothing.

So where do you begin? What's the best way to approach a man?

You don't just go up to a man and say, "Hi! Here I am—take me home." And if you do decide to approach a man, what do you have to walk up to him with? If you're in a restaurant you better make sure that food's not fallin' out of your mouth. Also, check for crumbs in your cleavage and lettuce in between your teeth. And if you've been drinkin', make sure your tits ain't lopsided and your hair weave ain't about to fall off.

Try to have a decent conversation. Don't come up with some "pick-up" line—but if you do, make it creative, and don't start talking astrology and sun signs!

Whether you're approached or you do the approaching doesn't really matter. But again, the one thing you don't want to appear to be is desperate. This doesn't mean that you can't send signals across the room with eye contact and your smile. Got to go to the bathroom? Use it as an opportunity to walk past him as you hold your head high and sashay by.

When you start talking, don't let everything out at once. Be a little mysterious, be someone who's going to make him wonder and want to know more about.

HOW TO ACT WHEN YOU MAKE CONTACT

Besides not looking and acting desperate, the most important thing to remember is your sense of confidence. When you're confident you know when to talk and when to shut up because some of you Girlfriends just babble away. Be a part of the conversation, but don't dominate it. Arrogance is when you think you're the finest thing on two feet and don't have to be considerate of anyone else's feelings.

There's a big difference between the two:

Confidence is "I trust me and I believe in myself."

Arrogance is "I don't trust none of you-all and I don't believe in nothin' all of you say . . . and I know everything while you don't know crap from apple butter!" (Yeah, they look a whole lot alike, and there's a whole lot of people who can't tell the difference between crap and apple butter, and I feel for 'em.)

WHAT TURNS MEN OFF WHEN YOU MEET THEM?

Desperation.

Pretentiousness.

Men don't like a phony chick.

Especially a desperate and phony chick.

And then to be desperate, phony, and ugly—and you "stank"?

(Cheap perfume usually won't blend with your body chemistry, so you "stank." Nothin' worse than thinkin' you're smellin' good when in truth you "stank"! Okay?)

Bottom line? Be honest and be yourself. Now, I'm not saying you shouldn't look good—nothing like embellishing and exaggerating what God gave you. But don't go so far overboard that you're out-and-out lyin', especially lies you can get caught in.

GIVE THE WEIRD ONES A CHANCE—JUST DON'T MEET IN THE CEMETERY

The worst places to meet men are in nightclubs, bars, restaurants, at weddings, and in cemeteries. Okay?

In nightclubs they're all lookin' and they're all lookin'

36

desperate. And there are lots of Girlfriends hangin' out with no panties—not even in their purse!

For fun I use to go into a bar and flirt with all the men. I would go in, tease them all, and work the room. I'd talk my talk to these dunderheads, none of whom I'd want to spend the rest of my life with.

My "cherry story" would work all the time:

> Me: "Hey, bartender, float me a few cherries
>   'cause I don't have one anymore. You
>   wanna take a bite of my cherry?"
> Dunderhead: "Sure. . . ."

Now, these are men I wouldn't even spend a quarter on to call them a cab, but it did wonders for my ego!

I used to go to this club in Cleveland that had happy hour and was geared for the white-collar working class. Everyone wore suits and ties, but I could always tell which guys really had jobs.

THE REAL DEAL BILL—OR PERPETRATOR PETE?

The Real Deal Bill had wrinkled shirts, jacket sleeves had creases, pants would have creases from sitting and walking. Perpetrator Pete had just put that sucker on an hour before—shirt crisp and clean, no ring around the collar yet! Aw, poor baby—trying to impress and find a woman who would support him.

I think it's wrong for a man to come into a bar with a suit on when he drives a truck for the water department. Why not come in wearing work clothes? It's honest. But because so many people are either afraid of rejection or are

♥

37

♥

just plain dishonest, you better really question a man before you believe what he's telling you.

> Me: "So, what do you do for a living?"
> Suit: "I'm a consultant."
> Me: "Well, who are you consultin'? Where do you work?"
> Suit: "I work out of my home."
> Me thinkin': Right—you ain't consultant nothin' but Pay Less to get you another pair of shoes.

❤
38
❤

Girlfriend, you can't be a stupid woman and go into a bar and believe everything you're told is the truth. Men who hang out in bars at happy hour usually have an agenda. And the agenda probably involves getting something and giving nothing. If a man is looking for a lifetime mate, his happy ass ain't gonna be in no bar!

❤   ❤   ❤

Personal ads? Another sign of desperation. You don't know enough people who can hook you up with somebody, you can't go out and get enough information on your own? You got to put an ad in the paper to advertise for a man? Get outta here! Call me. Mother Love will hook you up with one of her friends.

There are so many papers with so many ads, which tells me that there are so many desperate people in the world. There's plenty of room for Mother Love to help fill up the void.

You wanna meet a man?

Don't look, sound, or act desperate, which means don't put that ad in the paper.

❤   ❤   ❤

And the cemetery?

Why would you even think about meeting someone in a place full of dead people? You don't have much of a chance of coming across anyone who is alive, anyway. There was a guy who tried to pick me up one Memorial Day at the cemetery where my daddy and grandaddy are buried. I was busy cleaning off their graves and he's trying to hit on me.

> Me: "Fool! We're in a cemetery. Get out of
> here—this is a place for dead people!"
> Now, he was weird and creepy anyway.

❤

39

❤

But a word about the weird ones you meet: sometimes they can be the gems! A guy might seem a little "nerdy." He may be a little too big, doesn't dress exactly perfect, wears strange shoes, has funny hair, sweaty hands. But don't be so quick to look the other way. You may want to give the weird guy a chance.

Sometimes they can be the absolute best because so few women have given them the time of day and they really appreciate what love is supposed to be about. Girlfriend, if you can get beyond whatever is weird, you may have found a man who will spoil you and pamper you and wouldn't think twice about kissin' your drawers!

It's better to have one who loves you than one who don't.

Girlfriend, give the weird ones a chance—just don't meet 'em in the cemetery!

HOW I MET MY HUSBAND AND STARTED OUR RELATIONSHIP THAT HAS LASTED TWENTY-THREE YEARS

I met my husband at college. We were living in some of the first coed dormitories on the Big Ten campus of Ohio State University.

Our suites were in the tower. Me and my Girlfriends were sitting in the lobby playing "Rate a Dude." As the guys got off the elevators we would rate them. I was the commentator.

> Girlfriend: "Okay—he gets a seven."
> Me: "Why he get a seven?"
> Girlfriend: "He got a nice butt—but little feet so probably little wanker."
> Me: "Okay, movin' on . . ."
> Girlfriend: "He get a ten. Ooooh, look at that body and those big feet, gotta have a big one there!"

Then this man stepped off the elevator and I said, "Forget all that! There is my husband. He's gonna be my man."

This was the first time I had ever seen him.

But I knew he was my Hershey's kiss.

My own personal lifelong chocolate drop that I could suck on forever.

I got off the bench and cut him off between the elevator door and the steps to the cafeteria and threw myself on the floor spread-eagled in front of him and told him, "I am gonna be your wife! I wanna be your woman! Take me! I wanna bear your children and be your love!"

All right.

Now I gotta not only eat crow, but I gotta put ketchup on it.

I looked, acted, and sounded D-E-S-P-E-R-A-T-E!

And I was.

But only for him.

And I had my panties on.

My Girlfriends were in shock. They were just screamin' because they couldn't believe I did that. This man looked down at me and I looked up at him. We made eye contact and then I was lickin' my lips and closin' my eyes and spreadin' my legs.

Here he is getting off the elevator nonchalant and I, a complete stranger, fall on the floor in front of him. He stepped over me, backed up to the door, opened up the door, and ran down the steps so fast that it wasn't even funny!

Girlfriends are screaming, "What did you scare that dude like that for? That was wrong. You better leave him alone. He's real sweet and real quiet."

Me: "That's gonna be my man."

Girlfriends: "Leave him alone, leave him alone!"

Me: "That's gonna be my man, so all you chicks stay away from him. I'm tellin' you that he's mine!"

From that moment on I was on a mission. One of the girls on the bench playing the game was my suite mate and had gone to high school with him. Of course I wanted to know everything about him.

After that, he would come down to her room twice a week to get his hair braided. As she braided his hair, he would just sit and stare at me, smile, and not say a word. For at least a month I never heard him speak.

One weekend he came down to our suite. Everyone was gone except for me. He knocked on the door and he spoke, "Hello there."

> Me: "Ooooh, it's you. Come on in. . . ."
> He: "I'm lookin' for your girlfriend."
> Me: "Well, she's not here. They all went out. I'm here by myself. What can I do for you?"
> He: "I just came to get my hair braided, and she's gone?"
> Me: "Well, I'll braid your hair. . . ." (This was the first time I ever got him between my legs!)

He sat on the floor and draped his arms around my knees as I braided his hair. He fell asleep on my thigh, so peaceful. I woke him up after I finished and he left.

In college people slept together, and often not for sex but just as a togetherness kind of thing. There were always extra people in my suite because my suite was a safe place. My room promised a clean bed and a decent meal from my hot plate.

My future husband and I started sleeping together— he had and still has the best body temperature I've ever felt in my life. He was my personal blanket, a second skin. We kept sleeping together—*but all we did was sleep.*

After a month, I thought maybe he didn't like girls. You know how we can "go there." If a man doesn't jump your bones right away, you start thinking something is wrong with him. Girlfriend, I was no different.

One weekend everyone was gone from the suite and I decided to pamper myself. As a treat I had bought a hot pink nightie with satin and lace panties to sleep in. I had my foot on the chair, painting my toe dots, when I felt someone was watching me. I bent over and looked between my legs, through the lace edge of my panties, and saw my future husband standing against the door. Girlfriend, he was slobbering like the wolf who was about to have the Three Little Pigs for dinner.

Me: "What are you doing, standing there like
  that?"
He: "I'm just enjoyin' the view. . . ."

At last we had our beginning.
My panties came off.
And we've been at it ever since.

*Now Girlfriend, I ain't sayin'
you've gotta be a maid.*

But some good wifin' . . .

. . . *goes a long way.*

Mother love ©

CHAPTER THREE

*Never buy a man a pair of shoes, 'cause he'll walk
away in those same shoes.*
—My Mother

❤ ❤ ❤

9 told my future husband that I got to have a hip man,
that he's got to look good. Thank God he cleans up real
nice. Once we got together I helped turn him into a fashion
plate because he was looking like "hell movin'."

Of course you can take this too far. My mother had
warned me. She used to say:

"Baby, if you find a man in overalls, leave him in overalls! If you start puttin' him in a three-piece suit he's gonna
expect it.

"Don't ever spend no money on no man who's not
spending money on you. *And* . . .

"Never buy a man a pair of shoes, because he'll walk
away in those same shoes!"

My mother was right again. Before we were married
I'd bought him at least five pair of shoes and he had left

me five times. And just when I'd get used to him being gone, he'd come back.

> Me: "Now, what are you doin' back here? I
>   thought you'd walked away for good. . . . I
>   wanna get me a new boyfriend!"
> He: "No, you ain't gettin' no new boyfriend.
>   I'm your man. Period."

Yep, five pairs of shoes.

Yep, he left me five times.

And all together he was gone for five years in the sense that he had his own place . . . and a girlfriend, which I had to accept and could accept because I knew she'd never last.

Why? Because I knew she was no competition. She wasn't even a worthy adversary. He wanted to sow his wild oats, so he sowed 'em on a dunderhead. Why worry about that? (Oh Lord, did she dress bad! Where were the fashion police then?) And I was at his place every weekend that his girlfriend wasn't there, doing what I had always done: being irresistible!

WHATEVER YOU DO TO GET A MAN YOU GOTTA DO TO KEEP A MAN

How did I make myself irresistible to him? Shortly after I had thrown myself down on the floor in front of him, I became friends with his girlfriends to find out what they liked about him and what he liked about them. And then I did the total opposite and found out what he really wanted from a woman.

This man wanted an ambitious, strong woman who

could speak for herself, speak up in general, and who was full of fire. *But* that didn't mean he didn't expect some serious "wifin' "!

My husband comes from a family of five women who spoiled him rotten. When we first dated (until I caught on about the "wifin' " thing), I refused to cater to his domestic needs.

> Me: "I ain't ironing your shirts—do I look like your mama?
> He: "No, 'cause my mama would iron my shirt, my sisters would cook for me. . . ."
> Me: "Then take it off and let your mama and sisters do it!"

47

He did not find my attitude about these domestic issues appealing. That was when I had to weigh my own beliefs against what was really important to him. He meant so much to me that I was willing to compromise. I would do what his other liberated girlfriends wouldn't do. At first I was annoyed. But after a while I started to enjoy it. It stirred up something very primitive in me; and I began feeling things I'd never experienced before. What I was doing for him made me his woman. And the fact that he would receive it made him my man.

On an everyday, "untrendy" level I was giving a part of me (my time and my energy) without expecting anything in return. I was just doing what needed to be done.

I started cleaning his room, doing his laundry, and ironing his shirts. But, most importantly, I was a young woman who could cook. Many young women didn't or wouldn't cook in the early '70s. And I not only cooked, but I made everything from scratch.

I would take the flour, sugar, eggs, and butter and throw it together and make cakes. My future husband thought that this was absolutely fascinating. The other girls he was spending time with would not do any of the "wifin' " stuff he required. And while they matched his quiet personality, they didn't have the fire and passion he wanted.

Yes, I gave him everything he wanted while still being *me*. This made me infinitely irresistible. He had no choice but to love me—good-bye other girlfriends!

And I never wavered—whenever and wherever we were together he could expect: a clean home, good meals, me looking my best most times, me always ready to see him (whether it be accidental or on purpose), and my excellent hygiene habits—which must be stressed.

48

Girlfriend, as I told you before, if you wanna keep a man keep yourself clean enough to eat off of at all times. There's nothing worse than pulling your panties off and you get a whiff of odor that tells ya you need an "odor eater" down there. This sounds raw, I know. But I've heard Boyfriend say to Girlfriend, "Oh baby, what's that smell? Better put your panties back on!"

Or, you could be down on the floor and playing with your kids as they're scramblin' between your legs. One is sure to say, "Oooooooh, Mommy! We havin' fish for dinner?"

Many women make the mistake of thinking, Well I'll keep myself lookin' and smellin' fine . . . but once we move in together I can look like "hell warmed over" 'cause I got him!

Excuse me?

I don't think so.

Even if you never buy your man a pair of shoes, what you do to get a man you gotta do to keep a man.

Why should you put somebody you love through this?

It's bad enough that we all wake up in the morning looking like we're gonna bite! But to stay this way all day long is the worst thing you can do.

Check out this scene: He comes home. You're still in your old nightgown, lying around, haven't even gotten up and washed your face, and are looking more like a slug than a human being.

And, you're complaining, Girlfriend? You're complaining that he doesn't have time for you?

> Girlfriend: "I don't know why he don't want to
>   talk to me. . . . He don't find me attractive
>   no more."
> Me: "Well, I'm a woman and I can see why he
>   doesn't find you attractive. Get your butt
>   up and comb your hair and wash your
>   face and put on some lipstick—what's
>   wrong with you?"
> Girlfriend: "Well, he's my boyfriend."
> Me: "So just because he's your boyfriend means
>   he should have to look at a frumpy mess
>   of a woman?"
> Girlfriend: "Well, I'm too fat!"
> Me: "Well, if you feel too fat take your big ass
>   and get on a diet."
> Girlfriend: "Well, I'm too skinny and can't find
>   clothes that fit me. And I don't have no
>   money."
> Me: "Borrow a sewing machine and quit with
>   the complaining."

Complaining is easy. It's convenient. It's much easier to say I don't want to do this or that than to take a positive action.

And if your man does leave you for another woman, if he goes off with another big, fat chick, I'll bet she's a clean one!

MOTHER LOVE'S LOVE TEST

During our five-year "shoe romance," other girlfriend and all, I did a whole lot of thinking about what it takes to be sure that the man you love is really the one for you. I'm not talking about a whirlwind love affair; I'm talking about ten, twenty, thirty, forty years of togetherness and all the stuff and nonsense those years bring with them. During that period in my life and through the years of giving Mother Love advice, I developed my Mother Love Love Test. It's to help out all you Girlfriends before you wholeheartedly commit to a relationship and "give it all up" because you have a man. Yeah, I know, there are no absolutes, but what follows has helped the thousands of people I have dosed with Mother Love comfort.

Okay. Ready, Girlfriend? First a list of things to check off once you've discussed them or discovered the answers. And then we'll have some chitchat:

> 1. Ask him about his childhood. Where did he grow up? How many brothers and sisters does he have? Does he have a favorite one and if so, why? See if he opens up. If he's anxious to share family memories, chances are good that he'll share his feelings with you. If not, he'll probably shield his feelings.

> 2. Check out his folks! Of course you'd love to meet his parents! (That will really show you if he's screwed up and if so how bad: observe the

dynamics between his mother and father if possible. Remember, this has been his example of married life for years. And is he a mama's boy? And, how does he feel about dad?)

3. Any mental illness lingering in the family? Any crazy old aunties preaching out the back door to the air? Any uncles running naked down the street, just to feel free?

4. In our *age of plague* you must ask him about any sexually transmitted diseases he has or may have had—if you lose eye contact at this point I wouldn't believe everything he tells you. This means you should start discussing the issue and what it means to him, you, and both of you if you're headed in that direction. And if you are, make sure he wears a jimmy hat!

5. How does he look? Is he well groomed? Does he smell nice? Does his skin look clean? Are his hands well groomed? Check him out from head to toe each time you see him and look for consistency in his personal grooming habits. They shouldn't change.

6. If you're to the point of S-E-X, before you begin suggest a sexy bath and you'll learn a lot about his hygiene habits. Look inside his ears and a few other hard-to-see places.

7. How does he feel about kids? Don't trust a positive answer—"create a scenario." Arrange to have a couple of your friend's kids over when

you know he's coming to see you. How does he react? If he's perturbed, that will tell you kids aren't in his area of interest. But if he gets down on the floor and starts playing, he is either doing a great job of acting or really likes kids.

When I'd tell a boyfriend that I used to be a camp counselor I'd get one of two responses:

"I ain't got the patience!" or "Oh, I bet that was really nice—I'd love to have a houseful of kids."

8. Ask him if he'd like to go to church or synagogue with you. If he says he doesn't go, ask him why. If he tells you it's because he doesn't believe in God, I'd say good-bye. If he has an excuse like "Sunday Football," remind him that early service begins at 8:00 a.m.

9. Is he politically minded? Does he vote? Is he liberal or conservative? How does he feel about the community he lives in? Does he get involved to make it a better, safer place? (Or is he adding to the problem?)

10. Ask him about his favorite fruits and favorite colors. If he likes bright, vibrant colors and exotic fruits he probably has an outgoing personality and is open-minded.

A man who answers "I like blue, black, brown, and gray" is probably shy and may be moody.

11. Finally, play a game of twenty questions that reflect interests that *you have, your needs*. This will give you a good indication of compatibility. For

instance, if you like to travel ask him what his favorite country is and why. Other questions:

What are his favorite foods?
What are his favorite animals?
Which is his favorite holiday?
Which is his favorite season?
What's his favorite kind of car?
Does he prefer city life or country life?
Which is his favorite room in the house?
What is his favorite sport to play and to watch?
Does he like to read or would he rather go to the movies?
Does he like to shop?
What gets on his nerves?
Is there anything he can't tolerate?

Mind you, these questions can go on and on. And they can be very useful in building a relationship. Shoot, I wish I had taken this test and used the information I got when I first met my future husband. It would have made my life easier. Even Mother Love keeps on learning.

Now some quick chitchat about his clothing, in general. Why? I think it really matters because it demonstrates pride and self-respect—and also probably because I've been a clothes horse since I was fourteen!

A man who wears plaids and paisleys spends time coordinating his wardrobe. Clothes are important to him. But if he's got on a "loud" paisley shirt with bright plaid pants, he needs to go home and try again.

Tasteful silk ties tell me he's more conservative than a man who wears bow ties. Bow ties show humor and a quirky personality.

Suspenders are a whole 'nother trip! Yeah, suspenders can say "power," but to me they look ridiculous. They make a guy look like he's trying to keep his butt up: is it going to fall off, or what? To me, suspenders are an old-man thing!

Okay: Shoes!

You can't look neat if your shoes look beat!

Ragged-ass shoes?

Soles comin' loose?

I'd rather see a fifteen-year-old pair of quality shoes on a man than cheap shoes. Same holds true for his clothes. If I was your mama I wouldn't want you bringin' no raggedy-ass, soleless man home to meet me! Period.

54 GIRLFRIEND-TO-GIRLFRIEND TIPS

• No matter how much you love him, you can't make him love you. That's not to say you can't knock yourself out trying. . . .

• If you wake up one morning next to a man who you can no longer tolerate or stand, clean yourself up, get yourself together, *and* move on! (I'm not talkin' about "morning breath," but emotional or physical abuse.)

• Romance without finance is a nuisance!

• In any relationship, trust is a must!

• An angry woman is a lonely woman.

• Don't ever get involved with anyone who has more problems than you do.

• If it don't fit don't force it! (Use your imagination here.)

• Really get to know him before you plunge in headfirst. If he's secretive, watch him carefully. If you're secretive, watch yourself.

• Don't ever fall for this one—and if it's asked, I've got the answer for you:

Him: "Baby, I'm havin' a little cash-flow
    problem. Can you help me make my car
    payment?"
Your answer: "Excuse me, you were making
    your car payments before you met me,
    right? Do I have F.O.O.L. stamped on my
    forehead?"

• Be realistic:
    Girlfriend who's a waitress in a fast-food restaurant says, "I want to find me a man who makes a hundred thousand a year, has two BMWs, and likes fine wine!"
    Girlfriend, I hate to tell you but this kind of guy ain't gonna be checkin' out no waitress to be his girlfriend for anything serious—*it's only in the movies.*

• Beware of the "big spender" flashin' money so fast before your eyes that you're seein' green. Chances are good that he doesn't really have it and once it's gone he'll look to you. Using cash to flash smells P-H-O-N-Y!

55

• If he spends more time getting ready to go out than you do, he probably thinks that he's prettier than you. I always say, *Give me a man who can get dressed and pressed in twenty minutes!*

• Stay away from the naggers who complain about the amount of time you take to get beautiful. One of the worst fashion questions from a man? "Why ya gotta change your clothes fifteen times?"

• Beat-up cars are not too good to date in, but they don't have to be brand-new, either. I got into a car one time with this dude and cockroaches climbed out of the glove compartment. He was fine—but his car? I said I'd be goin' on the bus, and he was welcome to join me. He chose the cockroaches.

• Always keep some cab fare tucked in your bosom (I call mine the "Twin City Bank") 'cause you never know what the evening is going to bring, especially during the early stages of dating. He may drink too much and be too out of control to drive home.

• Conversely, don't let a man make you lose control by feeding you drinks or drugs. Know your limitations and don't go overboard.

For me, personally, one drink gets me drunk, two drinks have me six sheets to the wind, and three drinks have me singing on the table. I hold my liquor about as well as my auntie who took off her panties—enough said.

• I know from experience that you do not starve yourself all day for a dinner date because when you go out on that date you're going to want to eat everything in sight. Boyfriend will classify you as either a pig or a war orphan.

• Before you go out that door remind yourself of who you are, what you do, what you are about, *and never forget your purpose.* . . . Don't let a handsome face make you forget all of this.

GETTING IN THE GROOVE WITH ONE ANOTHER

Okay.

Hopefully you took my Love Test when you first started dating and have the advantage of knowing what I didn't know when I chased my future husband. Yeah, I chased him. . . .

Things are gettin' serious and it's obvious that there's something chemically going on here between the two of you—you've made his "thang sang" and you now know that you can sing soprano. The "oooh, baby"s have been never ending.

But beyond all that great sex and those good times, you have to learn to coexist, to find that common ground, because you're going to have dumb days.

Life is full of dumb days: no passion, no surprises, a kid is sick, you have your period, he's had a bad day at work, the sink's stopped up, he forgot to stop at the store on the way home, you shrank your favorite sweater, and you're mad at your mother so when he walks in the door you scream at him what you wish you'd told your mother when you'd had the chance.

Dumb days.

Dumb days when you do dumb things.

Dumb things that you wish you could take back.

Dumb days, nothing days.

These days end with his back turned to you with barely a kiss and a brief good-night.

Dumb days occur regularly in life and in all relationships. But they don't last forever, and chances are good that if it's dumb today it will be okay tomorrow. When I'm having a dumb day, I do my best to do something nice for myself or for someone who is having a dumber day than me. And if my husband turns his back to me at bedtime, I make sure I kiss him, hug him, and say a sincere good-night. Even if he doesn't respond exactly as I like, I can go to sleep without being angry. This is what works for me, and for my husband.

58

❤ ❤ ❤

So you know the reality of new shoes and old shoes, you've taken the Mother Love Love Test, I've shared some of my Girlfriend tips, and you know about dumb days. Now what?

You're together as a couple but nothing has been written in stone. Your not making wedding plans, but you know you want to be together—so how do you make it work?

The most important thing for you to remember is that no two relationships are ever the same, just as no two individuals are ever the same. Should you play hard to get? Not at this point in the relationship—you're beyond that. But that's not to say you can't still be a bit mysterious and unpredictable.

It's time to say "What Will It Take to Make This Relationship Work?" What can we do to make us strong as a couple? I can give you a few words to think about seriously that you can put into action when the bottom seems to be falling out:

Trust
Mutual Respect
Compromise
Pride
Sacrifice
Unconditional
Open-minded
Vulnerability
Faith
Love
Kindness
Hope

♥

♥

It's never easy, and it never will be easy. My husband and I have been together for twenty-three years and we're still learning about each other. And yes, from time to time, we will purposely push each other's buttons—overreact and get a little crazy—so we can pull "attitude."

We let the tension build like a thunderstorm, and when this storm finally hits, the release is so sweet that we can barely remember what all the fuss was about in the first place.

Sounds good?

Oh, baby, it is! But don't let anyone ever fool you—all relationships take work on every level of your being to keep them alive.

People are precious.

Especially boyfriends and husbands.

GREAT EXPECTATIONS

Besides the shoes I bought him, it took my husband and I thirteen years to get married for a couple of reasons. One was that he had a case of the "but"s instead of the "and"s— and, Girlfriend, you know how I feel about this!

He would say, "I love you *but*:

you talk too much;
you're too loud;
you cuss too much.

My future husband loved me with conditions and had great expectations. This didn't work for me because he was not accepting me for who I was when I was already very all right with who I was. While he realized I was comfortable with me, there were times when I was just too overwhelming for him. And he felt that I was so gregarious that he could not control me.

Outside influences were another part of our thirteen-year courtship. His fraternity brothers couldn't figure out why he was with me. I was too loud, too fat, too this, and too that. And his parents thought that I was the worst person in the world. How could he possibly degrade and desecrate their family by bringing home such a loud woman? My conversations with them would often go something like this:

His father: "I can't believe her! She's always
mouthin' off! Oh, no! All that back talk!
That's no way to act in this family."
Me: "Excuse me. Your son and I have sex. I
can talk back to him! He ain't my daddy.
And you sure ain't my daddy!

My husband grew up in a family where whatever his father said was the law. Nothing was up for discussion. This was not how Mother Love was raised!

I grew up without a father and my mother ran the household like a totalitarian dictator, but she also allowed us to voice our opinions. We could say what we really thought. She allowed us to develop as individuals.

My husband wasn't allowed to play with anyone besides his six other brothers and sisters. My mother always told us to go out and get our own friends—and at the same time we were to look out for one another. "Don't let anybody hurt them, and yet it's important that you have your own friends." We were raised in an open environment.

Mother used to say we could each have one friend over—well, hello! There'd be twelve kids scrambling everywhere before you knew it because there were six of us. I always had the most friends and I'd hear my brothers and sisters whispering, "Well, she's got five friends over here. That means we can't have any. . . ."

> Me: "Well, you-all ain't got no friends. Don't
> be mad at me 'cause I'm more popular and
> I'm cuter than all of you-all. Don't hate
> me 'cause I'm beautiful, okay?" (I learned
> these lines from my older sister.)

My mother was not a very physically affectionate person, and yet I knew what it felt like to hug my mother. I knew what it felt like after a bad day to have her be there. I could crawl up into my mother's lap and no matter how busy she was I could always lay my head down . . . provided she wasn't busy kicking my butt!

I knew what it was like to have Girlfriend talk with

61

my mother. I knew what it was like to share secrets with
her that she wouldn't tell the others—that is 'til I found out
that she was telling them everything anyway! And, eventually, the older my sisters and I got, the closer we became
as women.

My husband didn't grow up in this kind of environment, which I believe is a privilege and feel should be cul-
tivated in all families. Maybe that was why my husband's
vocabulary was filled with so many "but"s.

Grown up, when I would get nervous about performing, my mother would say, "People are going to always
want to make things more difficult, trying to smother your
uniqueness with their "but"s.

I'll never forget my first performance as a stand-up
comedian—I was a nervous wreck. I have never gone to
the bathroom so much in my life.

Girlfriend bet me fifty dollars that I wouldn't be able
to walk into the local bar, get up in front of strangers, and
make them laugh.

Me: "You're on!"

I had no idea that our local bar was a biker bar. I was the
darkest thing in there besides the leather they were all
wearing. When I stood up before all these redneck, leather-
clad, tatoo-wearing, hairy bikers (and these were the
women), I was terrified. I didn't know what to say, what to
do. I had really put my foot, shoe, and panty hose and all,
in my mouth.

This was my moment and I was stuck on stupid.
My mind went blank.
I could not leave.
I had no choice but to face my fear, so I started talking

back and forth with the audience. One guy in particular looked like he had a family of four living in his big old beard. Once he started laughing and joking with me, I was on and I took over. Damn, I was good!

I got a standing ovation and an invitation to come back as the weekend entertainment. Yeah, and I loved takin' Girlfriend's fifty dollars. I realized that there would always be times in my life when I would have to face my fears, when there was no place to run or hide. Once the fear is conquered, it ain't that serious, even though I spend a considerable amount of time in the bathroom before any performance.

When I shared my fears about performing Mother asked me:

"Is it difficult for you to go out on that stage?"

"No, ma'am."

"Is it difficult for the stuff to come through you that makes people laugh?"

"No, ma'am."

And then she'd grin and say, "Yeah, well that's because you're *my child!* What you have to do, baby, is just go out there *and* be your usual charming self, *and* you do what you want to do to be the best! You take them where you want to go; don't let them lead you.

"There are leaders *and* there are followers. I am your momma! *And* I'm the leader around here *and* I know I raised six more leaders!"

My mother knew about the power of *"and,"* and the great expectations it could help fulfill. Oh, my mother and her love.

Hallelujia!

*Husband and me in the middle of
our wedding/nightmare.*

*But even the good Pastor
Reverend Steinbeck couldn't slap
that happy grin off my face.*

CHAPTER FOUR

Hallelujah!
—Mother Love

❤   ❤   ❤

*L*et the church bells ring!

Mother Love and Boyfriend of thirteen years are getting hitched!

And it was a nightmare.

My wedding.

My wedding that I had started planning from the moment I saw this man get off the elevator in my college dormitory thirteen years before. I had waited patiently so many years for him to be ready.

It was a Sunday morning in November and we had moved in together *again* the year before. He had demanded that I "come home," enough of all this back-and-forth foolishness.

When I moved back in I had accepted that we would never be legally married. This was okay with me because if

I ever wanted to get up and "walk away" I could—and I didn't need no new shoes to help me out the door!

Yes, a Sunday morning in November. Since we weren't going to church we were cozy in bed. I was reading the paper and he was in a deep sleep. As I was reading the comics he woke up and said, "I wanna marry you."

Me: "Are you on drugs or what?"
He: "No, I'm wide awake. I really wanna marry you."

I didn't jump up and down and get excited.

I didn't scream and shout like I thought I would.

I didn't do the sanctified Hallelujah dance.

I didn't even cry.

Until that day he had never asked me to marry him—while I must have asked him fifty-seven times. He would always say, "Girl, you is trippin'—I ain't gonna marry you. No way. You don't do what I tell you to do."

Me: "But don't you love me?"
He: "Yeah, I love you—but aw, you ain't never gonna do what I tell you to do . . . uh-uh . . . and it's gonna be a problem."

We had been playing house for so many years—living in "sin"—and our son was seven years old. Why get married? So I looked at him straight in the face and said, "Call my mother and tell her that." I knew he would never lie to my mother.

He rolled over, picked up the phone, and called her up. "Hey! How you doin' this fine Sunday morning?"

My mother: "What's the matter? What's the
    matter?"
He: "Oh, nothing's the matter. I thought it
    would be nice for me to call and let you
    know I'm going to marry your daughter."

I heard a big thud through the phone and I jumped out of
bed and got dressed. When I arrived at my mother's house
she was dressed, pressed, and ready to go!

Fiancé's Mastercharge was in our hands (that way if
he changed his mind he'd have to pay), and that very same
day Mother and I went out and looked for a wedding dress.
We went to every store and every place that looked,
smelled, or sounded like wedding.

67

Because it had taken us thirteen years to get married,
I wanted my wedding to be an extravaganza! My Girlfriends
ranged in all sizes—from a size zero to a size fifty-four—
and the ones who were in my wedding were the ones who
were closest to me at this time in my life.

Girlfriends who I had known since I was a child and
many of my sorority sisters refused to be in my wedding
because they were jealous that I was getting married. But
they used the excuse of being upset with who I was marrying because of all the changes he had put me through.
And they'd start telling me about all these things that they
had seen him do, old girlfriends he was talking to, couldn't
understand why I loved him. They didn't seem to understand that this is what it took to create *our relationship*, a
relationship that could finally be blessed in marriage.

Me: "It's not for you to understand. It's not for
    anybody else to understand. All I'm asking

is for your support and to trust my
judgment. I'm not marrying a bad person."

Well, the Girlfriends that "hung with me" and I had the
best time planning this big event. But I had to tell them,
"Unless you all are forking over money to help me pay for
this, just go along with the program!"

My mother and I went to the annual bridal fair in
Cleveland. This was a big to-do, held at a swank, fancy
hotel for two days. The placed was filled with all kinds of
samples of wedding stuff and information: flowers, gowns,
and the best places to take your honeymoon.

And then there were all the "patterns" to pick from
for china and silver. Yeah, I looked at all of this, knowing
full well we was gonna be eatin' off of paper plates with
plastic! My version of china were the paper plates at the
grocery store—and I could pick out a different pattern
every week. And this way there was no need to do dishes.
Yes, we could continue to be happy eating off of paper
plates, using plastic utensils, and drinking from plastic cups.

So here we are, Mother and I, wandering through the
ballrooms as we absorbed all of this bridal splendor. I
started laughing and cracking jokes with this guy who was
wearing a red jacket and carrying a walkie-talkie. I thought
he was a cute little security guy. He kept following me as
I joked about everything I saw.

My mother was sitting in the auditorium waiting for
the fashion show to start and had reserved my seat, which
was three feet from the front of the stage. When I sat down
she asked, "Where you been?"

Me: "Oh, I've just been walking around doing
wedding stuff." I was carrying this big old
shopping bag full of wedding samples.

My mother: "Girl, this is gonna be a terrible
show! They have this man up here and
he's gettin' on my nerves!"

I look up and see this guy on stage before 5,000 women
who are waiting for bride tips. He was losing it as he said,
"Oh, God, I'm a disc jockey. . . . I talk to a microphone—
not to real people. I don't know what to do. . . . I don't
know what to say. . . ."

I said as loud as I could, "Shut up and give me the
microphone!" He was gettin' on my nerves, my mother's
nerves—and I had to keep my mother happy. Otherwise
she was liable to get up and start cussing everyone out and
I'd have to leave with my shopping bag over my head!

This poor man looked down at me and said, "What?"

The guy with the red jacket and walkie-talkie, who
was standing behind me and who I had assumed was a security person, started waving his hands, exclaiming, "Let her
go! Let her go! Let her get onstage!"

As the disc jockey handed me the microphone he
asked me my name. I said, "Baby, I'm Mother Love—just
give me the microphone and you go sit down while I talk
to all of these Girlfriends!"

I began: "How y'all doin'?
How's your mama doin'?
All right, babies, so you-all wanna get
married?
I'm gettin' ready to get married too!"

Then I stomped my foot and began singin' some silly little
song and did this whole wedding routine, talking back and
forth with the audience, while we were all waiting for the

fashion show to begin. The show was running late so I ended up doing twenty-five minutes of stand-up comedy.

After I did this routine I heard, "Okay, Mother Love—we're ready!"

> Me: "Okay, you-all. We gettin' ready to see
> some bride dresses now. When I see mine
> I'm gonna throw my hand up—so don't
> you-all buy that wedding dress!"

When I stepped off the stage they gave me a standing ovation. My mother was telling everybody within shouting range, "That's my daughter! That's my baby! Did y'all see my baby?"

> Me: "Ma, sit down. Oh God, Ma, sit down!"

She got out of her seat, disappeared into the aisles, and started telling everybody that she was my mother. She was the P.R. Queen! As she did this, the disc jockey and the man in the red jacket whisked me off into another room. It turned out that the disc jockey was a program director of a major radio station. And the guy in the red jacket with the walkie-talkie, who I thought was a security guard, was the promotional director for the radio station.

Once we were in the room, and they had found my mother for me, they said, "Your name is Mother Love?"

> Me: "Oh, yeah, that's what the babies call
> me—Mother Love."

They asked me if I would come back the next day. I told them I'd come back but my routine would be something new and different because I never knew what was going to come out of my mouth.

> My mother: "Oh, she can do it! She can do it!"
> Me: "Ma, you gonna come back down here tomorrow with me?"
> My mother: "Girl, no, I ain't comin' back. They all got on my last nerves—get your sisters and girlfriends!"

I agreed to come back if they would treat me and my bridal party to brunch—this meant me, my maid of honor, and my thirteen bridesmaids. Whatever I wanted they said I could have. When I called my bridal party, none of them believed me except my sister and my maid of honor.

Next day the three of us went to the hotel brunch. We took our time, ate up a storm, and drank mimosas until I was half-drunk. We strolled into the exhibit area, where they had all been waiting for me. They had security guards to escort me to the stage, whispering back and forth on walkie-talkies, "Ms. Love is here. Ms. Love is here."

I was introduced to everyone who was anyone as we walked to the auditorium. My sister started crying, "Oh my God, they're treating you like a star. This is like what we see on television. Oh my God, they've got walkie-talkies and everything!"

I had to turn around and slap her to bring her back to reality.

"Girl, shut up!"—POW!

Then my girlfriend is screaming, "Girl, we ate free. Girl, we got everything free. We park free—I love this already!" She was off and running for the perks!

By the time I got onstage I had a huge shopping bag

71

full of merchandise to advertise for the exhibitors. And I did another standing-ovation comedy routine. At the end, my sister was a wreck, still crying, "Oh, my sister!"

Before I left the bridal fair I was given everything a bride dreams of and I was thinkin', Oooh, some of this stuff I can pawn 'cause it's gonna be needing silver cleaner!

But, best of all, I got real dishes! I mean a whole big box full of china plates and china bowls and china everything. I eat off plastic only when I have to.

When I was finished with the exhibitors, all the "big cheeses" from the radio station said, "We want to put you on the radio, Mother Love."

Me: "Yeah, when the drugs wear off, call me!"

Girlfriend, let's pause for a moment and look at what's happened: Boyfriend has asked me to marry him and I get offered a job on the number-two rock-and-roll radio station in Cleveland while I'm at a bridal fair trying to plan my big, elaborate wedding and keep my mother happy.

Getting this job wasn't about being Black.

Getting this job wasn't about being a woman.

Getting this job wasn't about anything but being my usual charming self and fulfilling my purpose!

When all this happened I was a school-bus driver—morning pickup and afternoon drop-off. Shortly after the bridal fair, one day I dropped off all sixty-six of my kids at school, I went down to the radio station, and I signed a two-year contract that would allow me to make more money than I had ever made in my whole life.

Only Husband knows all my deep, dark secrets.

But he's still my lovable Biscuit Head.

CHAPTER FIVE

"Only virgins get white runners!"
—The Good Pastor Reverend Steinbeck

💜 💜 💜

The day I signed my contract with the radio station, I never picked up the kids. It was the most irresponsible thing I had ever done; for all I know these kids could still be at the Robert Fulton Elementary School waiting for their ride home!

Nobody believed what had happened until they heard me on the radio the next morning. I almost killed all the bus drivers and the kids!

All I had to do was come to the station daily and babble on the radio. I was like a sidekick for the station: in the morning I did "Dear Mother Love Letters" and in the afternoon I did the weather and sports.

What did I know about weather?

If it was going to be cold I'd say, "Put on some underwear."

Made sense to me.

But what about my wedding?

I had thirteen bridesmaids, two flower girls, two junior ushers, a ring bearer—and however many more people it took to make a wedding party of thirty-eight. My son was to carry the train behind my dress. He was too old to be the ring bearer and he didn't want to be no "junior usher" because, as he said, "The bride is my mommy, and my daddy is the groom, and I should have a big job!"

We sent out 585 wedding invitations and through the perks of my radio job I got:

> my wedding flowers for almost nothing;
> free wedding rings;
> free tuxedos for my husband-to-be and my son;
> beautiful gifts;
> and my virginal, snow-white gown with full cathedral
>   train for half-price.

75

The wedding was to take place at the Open Door Baptist Church. The minister who was going to marry us was the sweetest man. We had to go and see him a few times for some "premarital" counseling to make sure that we were really ready for the commitment of marriage.

After talking to us, he said, "You-all should of been married a long time ago. You two are more stable than people I know been married thirty years!"

We were to marry June 15, 1985. The wedding invitations were sent out and read: FINALLY THEY'RE GETTING MARRIED.

Friends called and said:

"We thought y'all were already married!"

"Didn't we come to your wedding at that old church?"

"Wait a minute—what about your son? I thought he had your husband's last name."

Me: "Don't mean squat! He has his last name.
The dog has his last name. Now it's my
turn to get it."

Two weeks before our wedding we found out that our sweet minister was going away on a surprise vacation the weekend we were to be married. It was a gift from his congregation.

Good-bye, Sweet Minister.

Hello, Pastor Reverend Steinbeck.

We should have had a clue that there could be problems when you've got a Black Baptist minister named Steinbeck. Okay? Work with me here, people.

When we met Pastor Steinbeck he was like one of those

Deep
southern
Baptist
ministers
who
talks
to
you
very
slowly
and
very
deeply
and
is

very
religious . . .
and he wants to preach to you right away!

Boyfriend and I are baffled—Steinbeck? How come he's not named Pastor Omar Jones or Reverend Green? Where did the "Steinbeck" come from?

From the very beginning Pastor Steinbeck had an attitude.

He asked us, "Is there anything you want me to do?"

(I felt like saying, "Change your name.")

I said, "Yes, sir."

Boyfriend is bumpin' me with his knee under the table to get me to shut up.

I continued, "Will you please wear a dress robe, because this is a full formal church wedding?"

♥

77

♥

He: "I ain't got to wear no robe. . . ."
Me: "But you asked, and this is what I would
        like."

Pastor Steinbeck's refusal to wear the robe was just the beginning of the nightmare, the beginning of the "hilarious" nightmare.

The man who I wanted to give me away, who was totally in love with my mother and who I actually called Dad, said he would be pleased to give me away. . . .

Me: "Here is where you go to rent a tuxedo."
Him: "I ain't wearin' no tuxedo. I ain't puttin'
        on somebody else's clothes."
Me: "But it's a full formal wedding."
Him: "Well I ain't wearin' nobody else's
        tuxedo!"

Me: "Well, I'll buy you a tuxedo."

Him: "I ain't wearin' a tuxedo to no wedding. I got plenty of nice suits!"

Me: "But, Dad, it's a full formal wedding. You'll look out of place without a tuxedo on. Will you at least wear a black suit?"

Him: "I ain't wearing no black suit. I got a nice blue suit."

Me: "But that will throw off everything in the wedding."

♥

78

♥

From this point on we got into a big argument and he didn't give me away. I had never asked him for anything until now. I was really hurt. So my uncle gave me away, which was a better choice anyway.

I spoke with my sisters about the food, and they just cussed me out. And when I asked my older sister to cook the food for the reception she said that was all I thought she was: "the cook." No, she wouldn't cook. And my sister can throw down! So my husband's best man's family got together and cooked the food for the reception, and did a wonderful job. And all my sisters did was complain about the food during the reception.

Okay? So where are we?

We got a Black Baptist pastor named Steinbeck who won't wear clerical robes.

A man I've been calling Dad who won't even wear a black suit to walk me down the aisle.

Sisters cussing me out and later complaining about the food that was prepared.

And on the day of our wedding it rained, and it rained, and it rained all day.

Oh, yeah, and we wanted to throw confetti and send up doves. But Pastor Steinbeck said no because the confetti would make a mess and there wouldn't be anyone to clean the bird "doo-doo" off the church. We were instructed just to walk out of that church and get into the car.

No fuss!

No mess!

And as far as Pastor Steinbeck was concerned, there would be no hoopla at all.

❤   ❤   ❤

So it's the Big Day!

My bridesmaids wore elegant two-piece dusty rose gowns and rings of flowers with big net bows in their hair. (Girlfriends weren't wearing no hats 'cause they were gettin' their hair done special for my moment.)

Ten minutes before the wedding my future husband's best man approached me and said, "He's not here, he said he wasn't comin' and he said he wasn't going to do this."

With my hands on my hips I told him, "You can take your lying self out of here. This is church and I'm not going to cuss you. Just get out!"

He: "You don't believe Brother ain't here?"
Me: "I know he's here. Maybe you don't want
      him to be here—but I know he's here."
      Dunderhead!

It was time to roll out the white runner. Pastor Steinbeck solemnly approached me and said, "Let's get started."

"Well, my white runner is not here. I've sent some-body to get it."

"You don't need no white runner! Only virgins walk

❤

79

❤

down the aisle on a white runner. You ain't no virgin. Girl, what's wrong with you?"

There was no way the wedding was going to start until I got a white runner, 'cause he wasn't gonna come back here and get in an argument with me, when I'd paid for the church, and him, and security. As far as I was concerned, he better get outta Dodge!

I had to have security because by this time I had become a local celebrity. The media was there to take pictures, but I told them they couldn't publish them. There was a big announcement in all the Cleveland newspapers and magazines that Mother Love was getting married! But I was still trying to keep my common foot with my common folk.

Now, this was a double-aisle church, and the groomsmen were to come down one aisle and the bridesmaids down the other aisle. They were to meet in the front, cross, and go to their places to make this huge wedding party.

Well, it came time for them to come out the door and I had attendants at both sides of the doors so that they could open up the doors for the bridesmaids—you could see the guys coming down the aisle in a line but the ladies had an entrance to make. Well, when the sixth bridesmaid made her entrance (I'm back there coordinating everyone), Pastor Steinbeck said as loud as he could, "Well, are they ever gonna stop coming out that door? Well, how many peoples be in this weddin'? Why you got to have all these people in here? What's wrong with y'all?"

I told the rest of the bridesmaids, "Hurry on up! Get down that aisle, just get on down there before I have to kill him."

We had silk flowers made for the bouquets because I,

my mother, my brother, and my son are all serious hay-
fever sufferers. I had a huge bouquet of silk white roses,
white tiger lilies, and baby's breath. But I left my whole
bouquet behind because I had to get down the aisle before
I killed Pastor Steinbeck.

As my Uncle and I and my son got ready to come
down the aisle, full cathedral train on my dress and all, four
of my old boyfriends were in the back of the church
screamin', "Don't do it! Don't do it! Don't marry him—what
we gonna do? Well, at least we seen what he looks like—
she ain't marrying no ugly dude." They were makin' a ruckus
and fannin' themselves!

Here I was, at the back of the church waiting for the
music to begin, and I said, "Shut up. . . . Uncle, get them
out . . . stop the clownin'!" But we couldn't help laughing.

Girlfriend, when the bridal march started and we
started down the aisle, my old boyfriends stood up and
started cheering like they were at a football game. No light
applause, but down-and-out foot-stompin' as they screamed,
"Go! Go! Go!" They were so loud that you couldn't even
hear the wedding march.

I dragged my uncle down the aisle as my son followed
with my train. I had told the good Pastor Steinbeck that
my husband was a "southpaw," so I would be standing on
his left side instead of his right side.

After we had taken our positions Pastor Steinbeck told
me to move to the right side. I started to move and then
said, "No, I'll stand on the left because he's left-handed."

Pastor: "No, you stand on the right side. . . ."

Well, Girlfriend, I'm being moved back and forth and
back and forth. My son got so mad that he slammed the
train of my gown down on the floor and said, "When you

decide where you're gonna stand, I'll pick your dress up!"
He sat down in the first pew, folded his arms, and said,
"Okay?"

All I could think was what a fiasco my dream wedding
had become. Pastor Steinbeck finally began the ceremony:

"Dearly
beloved,
we
are
gathered
here
today
before
God
to
unite
this
man
and
woman. . . . Why you got on a white dress? What you
doin' in white? You ain't no virgin! You got a son big as
me sittin' over there. What you got all these people doin'
in your wedding? I bet you spent a bunch of money for
this—and you-all ain't gonna stay married for six months.
See, that's what's wrong with you young people—you come
in here today, you just think it's all dress-up, look real
pretty, and wear a white virgin dress. You ain't no virgin—
ain't none of you no virgins in here. Got all these children
in here desecratin' the church like this!"

Me: "Have you lost your mind? Look, I will be
in church for Sunday service tomorrow,
but you better shut up."

Husband-to-be snatched my hand out of the air, put my finger down because it was wagging while my other hand was on my hip, and I went into one of my Girlfriend stances. From the pews I heard a collective, "Oh, God. . . ."

Pastor Steinbeck had gone from "dearly beloved" to discussing my virginity. Husband-to-be said, "You take your hand off your hip, close your mouth, let the minister do the marryin'. . . ."

"But he—"

Husband-to-be was talkin' through his teeth. "Just calm down and take your hand off your hip 'cause we're about to marry."

Now husband-to-be turned directly to the pastor and said, "I do!"

"Well, I didn't even ask you nothin' yet!"

"Well, when you ask me I'm going to tell you 'I do'—so I *do!*"

"Well, let me ask you first."

Husband-to-be says, "Yeah, yeah, yeah—I do!"

Then the pastor spoke to me. "Well, Miss ah, Miss ah, Miss ah—"

I told him, "Ms. Love. Ms. Mother Love."

And he continued, "Miss ah, Miss ah—" I told him my name again.

Husband-to-be cut in again with his "I do."

"Well, I didn't even ask you that part yet!"

"Well, I'm tellin' you I'm gonna do it when you ask me, so just get on with it!"

We had asked Pastor Steinbeck to pronounce us "man and woman" or "husband and wife"—we didn't want "man and wife." The good pastor said, "I now pronounce you husband and wi—ma—and wi . . . I now pronounce you *man and wife!*"

Me: "That's not what I asked you!" (Husband
    pulled me to him, threw my veil up off
    my face, kissed me real hard, and then
    said to me, "Okay, let's go." I started
    crying as we walked down the aisle.)
Husband: "What are you crying for?"
Me: "Because I can't kick his butt in church. I
    think he should be whipped, flogged—
    something!"
Husband: "Let me get you out of here right
    now, because you actin' a fool."

Okay. So where are we now?

84

In front of 800 people (people had come who weren't
even invited) my virginity had been discussed.

I had arranged to have a videotape made and had
hired a photographer to take lots of pictures. When the
photographer gave me my wedding pictures they were all
double-exposed except for one—and it has a nick on my
husband's face. My mother insisted on buying the proofs,
double-exposed and all, because she said I should have my
wedding pictures.

The video guy never showed up because he didn't
have a cover for his video camera and didn't want it to get
wet in the rain.

Me: "Why can't you put the camera under your
    coat? You can't? Well, give me back my
    one hundred and twenty-five dollars!"
    (Never saw that money again.)

This was a nightmare wedding.

A mish-mash wedding on a hot, humid, sticky, rainy day.

Imagine the reception with 800 people.

Disc jockey, too, spinnin' the tunes!

But they all ate good, and drank good too. There was plenty of everything!

But somewhere between the bakery and the reception somebody stole the pastries and cakes. And guests were stealing the liquor. What wasn't stolen, my husband and his friends would polish off on the weekends—for months they got drunk every weekend while watching sports! Rather than get angry, I went along with these crazy weekends and did my "wifin'" thing as the cook!

This is how I kept my new husband home and happy.

This is how we got into the habit of having weekend parties at our house.

This was the beginning of our social life as a married couple.

And we've been married ever since.

Forget about prewedding jitters, because whatever can go wrong will go wrong. Yes, my wedding was a nightmare, but, in retrospect, a hilarious nightmare. And this is the way you should approach married life.

Ya gotta be tough enough to roll with the flavor, have a sense of humor, and realize that your life will continue to be filled with the good, the bad, and lots of Pastor Reverend Steinbecks.

Oooo, Girlfriend, now we're gonna get nasty.

No matter how much I rant and rave, he'll always be my chocolate drop.

❤ ❤ ❤ ❤ ❤ ❤ ❤ ❤ ❤ ❤

I am the Love Goddess of the Universe . . .

The Nefertiti of Naughtyness.

And you might learn some of my sizzlin' sex secrets!

Mother love ©

CHAPTER SIX

Get you an education so that you never need any of
them to do nothing for you—not even pay your rent.
Why, you don't even depend on a man for sex!
—My Mother

❤ ❤ ❤

*W*hoa!

Wait—time out!

What do you mean about this sex thing?

I've been looking forward to that.

Don't tell me this, Mother; this is not a good thing,
Mother.

I've been looking forward to the sex thing.

Come on! Help me with this!"

My mother used to say to me, "You don't have to
worry about a man satisfying you because they ain't never
gonna get it right 'cause they're always going to be concerned just about their own 'rocks.' Don't worry about nothing like that unless the battery company goes out of
business."

Me: " 'Scuse me?"

Ma: "When the day comes that Eveready puts
a sign up that says GOING OUT OF
BUSINESS then you better worry 'cause as
long as the factory is in business you can
get you a vibrator—why hell, as long as
there's electricity . . ."

I'm thinking, I don't even wanna be into toys. There has to
be a way around this attitude. Like I said before, Mother
was a serious male basher. When I was young our sex dis-
cussions would go like this:

❤

89

❤

Me: "How you gonna tell me about sex? You
can't get a man, you hate men, ya got six
kids—what would you know about sex?"

Ma: "Well, how in the hell do you think I got
six kids?"

Me, *thinking*: I don't know. . . . I ain't got a clue.
I think he must have muzzled you and
then gave it to you, but I sure don't know
what your problem is!

RETHINKING SEX

Everything I learned about sex, about pleasing a man and
myself, I discovered by trial and error. My mother and I
were on different wavelengths about many sexual issues—
but not about the topic of pleasure.

I was a hog when it came to men, okay? (And I still
am today with my husband!)

I thought that the purpose of men in my life was for

them to please me. Period. This is what I thought because this was what my mother told me.

> Mother. "If you're gonna be involved with a
> man it should be for your sole pleasure. If
> he can't do it for you get rid of him. You
> don't need him."

Now here is where our paths parted. Mother was telling me that men were for my sole pleasure, and I'm thinking, while she's talking, But what if you really like them? Do I have to get rid of them even if they can't do it too good? This was confusing because I really liked men at an early age. I liked being around them, I liked their company, the way they smelled, the way they felt—I even liked their conversations. (Yeah, these Biscuit Head men can talk crazy, but I still like having a conversation with them.)

I just didn't think that they could be as bad as my mother made them out to be. So I went on my own personal mission to find out just what men were all about. And in the process I found out that I'm just as good a friend to men as to women.

Girlfriend, we can have friendships with both sexes. All it takes on our part is an open mind and big ears for listenin'.

While we grew up in an all-black neighborhood, attended an all-black church, and were raised most of our lives by my mother, alone in the ghetto (my father died when I was nine), Mother never talked about racism.

Sexism, yes. Racism, no. And she didn't condone homosexuality, but she didn't condemn it, either.

Mother: "You have to do what you can live
with. . . ."

LET ME MAKE YOUR "THANG SANG"!

It's been twenty-three years. Twenty-three years of sexual peaks
and valleys with Biscuit Head Husband as my partner. This is
why I feel I can let you all know what works and what don't—
especially the "don't"s. So throw away all those sex books.

You know where to touch him, don't ya?

If you don't, ask him what he likes, what feels good.
We all have different sex zones. Those are the spots that
make you wanna scream, "Oh yeah, baby!"

And you show him where to touch you. You should
be in tune with your body, know what parts of your body
react to kisses and licks and sucking and stroking. Now I'm
starting to sound like Dr. Ruth or authors Masters and John-
son, and John Gagnon of *Sexual Conduct: The Social Sources of
Human Sexuality*. . . . Oh please, it ain't that deep. And I don't
agree with their statistics—they're way off!

Yes, we all have erogenous zones. But it's different
strokes for different folks. For instance, there's a place my
husband kisses me that's very exotic and erotic—and I ain't
saying where! (No, not *there*.) Why, he can kiss me there
and my panties are soaking wet just like that! Oh, my! He
can kiss that spot and just squeeze any part of my big booty
and I start to tingle.

FEELIN' GOOD

So where is it for you? What parts of your body respond
to his touch? No, besides those obvious places, Girlfriend!

Ears are a turn-on for some, but I know Girlfriends who can't stand to be kissed in their ears—they think it's gross and disgusting. Personally, it's too quick for me.

Some men like to lick armpits. Now, I don't have armpits because I had to have my sweat glands removed, which is a whole 'nother story. But I have Girlfriends who tell me that their husbands just love to lick their pits!

And men love to kiss *all* those clean-shaven places, above the waist and below the waist. Kissin' and lickin' those clean-shaven parts is mmmmm . . . good!

The bottom line for any of this pleasure is both of you being comfortable and knowing what you like and what you don't like. And this is what you gotta teach one another if you don't know.

It is about you knowing where you want to be touched and how you want to be touched. See, now I want to be hugged and squeezed hard. I've always liked this. Most men want to hug you delicately because they think you're gonna break. On the other hand, I am not so delicate that Husband is not afraid to slam down hard on me. Get the picture?

So put some foot in it, baby; let me feel you! Don't just hug me—collect me in your arms!

If your man is shy, do to him what you want done to you. Hopefully, he'll follow your lead. If you're both very, very shy, but if you've reached the point where you are both about to be very, very naked, you can't be that shy. You might be shy to the world, but this is where communication is so very important. Open up your arms, spread your legs, lie back and relax, knowing that what you are about to do is one of the most fulfilling and enjoyable experiences in our lives. And this is just the beginning—there are so many things that you can do with one another from this point on.

SEX CHATTER

Yeah, twenty-three years, and my husband is still very shy. But I talk sex talk to him all the time. Husband don't need no 900 number for sex talk!

One time we were in front of Kinko's—the photocopy center of L.A.—and I just had to give him a tease.

Me: "What if I were to grab you by your butt
　　and squeeze it and your wanker in front
　　of this store?"
Husband: "Ooooh—you're just so nasty!"
Me: "And you love it!"

93

We just laughed all the way into the store. People were lookin' at us like we were crazy or something. Instead of calling the copy center Kinko's, Husband and I call it "Kinky's"!

Now, as shy as my husband is, he's got a bit of the devil in him, too. One day we were standing on the street corner waiting to cross and he just ran his hand right up under my dress!

Me: "What are you doin'?"
Husband: "I just got an urge."
Me: "Okay! Go with it, baby—go with it!"

As I stepped off the curb people could see that his hand was sliding down my thigh and coming out from under my dress! He raised his hand and pointed to his wedding ring, like he was saying, "This is my wife and I can do this." Guys passing him gave him the high-five sign.

YOU HAVE TO BE YOUR OWN SEX THERAPIST AND SEX EXPERT

In our society we make the mistake of relying on supposed experts to tell us when to do it, how to do it, where to do it, which way to do it, and how it's going to feel. The reality is that we are all different. You are the only one who knows what works for you, and this is what you have to communicate to Husband or Boyfriend.

My needs and turn-ons are not the same as Dr. Ruth's or Erica Jong's (although I have a very real fear of flying). And what works for Mother Love is not necessarily going to work for you. I can't imagine Husband lickin' my armpits because I don't have them, and because he ain't an armpit-licking kind of guy. But I got a Girlfriend who tells me how her husband begs her not to wear deodorant after she showers because he wants to lick those pits.

Now, Girlfriend told me it doesn't do anything for her, but it's what he likes so she accommodates his desire. Fulfilling desires is something you should both do for one another as much as possible.

The great thing about the human body is that there are so many nooks, crannies, cracks, holes, and appendages to play with and explore. Personally, I will tell you my husband is the best-tasting man in the world for me. And I'll go the distance as long as he holds up!

MAKE A LIST OF WHAT YOU LIKE:

Whether it's:

Mirrors so I can watch our passion in action.
Flavored lubricants can be a lot of fun.

Satin sheets have been around forever, and for a good
   reason—talk about slip-sliding away!
Candles and incense and scented oils.
A bowl of fresh fruit by the bed.
Fresh flowers everywhere.

If he doesn't like deodorant or perfume on you, he needs
to tell you. Many men like to make love after a shower or
bath because they can taste and enjoy your fresh, clean
skin.

And here's something that we all can do with our part-
ners: both of you make lists of what you like and then swap
lists. If you're shy put it in an envelope and stick yours in
his briefcase or lunch bag.

95

What about his list for you? Think about what he's
shared and try to do at least one of the things that was on
his list the next time you make love. And of course, ideally
he'll do the same for you. I like doing this because it creates
a little spice in our sex life.

COLLECT YOUR PLAYTHINGS

Have on hand at all times votive candles, fresh fluffy towels,
terry-cloth bathrobes, incense, lingerie, crotchless panties,
garter belts, real silk stockings, fragrance, perfume, sensual
oils—and any of your favorite playthings. I have a Girlfriend who strokes her man with peacock feathers . . . up
and down and up and down. She keeps them in a vase
beside the bed.

Collect all these things so that when you want to set
the mood you don't have to be bothered about shopping—
especially if you're low on cash. So stock up!

MY SPECIAL RECIPE

I have two aphrodisiac drinks to share with you. One is a great relaxer before you make love and the other will cool you down after you have had some hot, steamy sex.

DRINK #1 (Before sex)
You need:
1 cup orange juice
Cinnamon sticks or powdered cinnamon
5 cloves
1 tbsp. lemon juice

♥

96

♥

     Put the cinnamon and the cloves in the bottom of the pan. Add the orange juice and heat it slowly. Now add that tablespoon of lemon juice. Let it all simmer on low until the aroma fills your kitchen. Pour it in a mug and sip it as you're getting ready for a date or looking forward to some quality time with your man. It will make you feel warm deep inside as it relaxes you.

     Now, you can add a little libation—a little brandy might be good—but I think it's better without alcohol. Too much alcohol can dull the senses.

DRINK #2 (After sex)
You need:
Strawberries or your favorite berry in season
Fresh pitcher of lemonade
Crushed ice

     Mix all the ingredients in your blender. Again, you can add a little libation and you can use as many kinds of fruits as you like. This is the best drink to sip, and there ain't nothin' like it on a hot night when you've just finished having some hot, steamy sex!

HOW OFTEN?

I would rather have really good sex once a week than mediocre sex every day. Not having an orgasm would worry me to death. I'd be like, "No way—you better get down and put your face in the place." When you don't have an orgasm you feel unfulfilled, frustrated, and usually carry a bad attitude for the rest of the day. So why waste your time?

♥
97
♥

If orgasms aren't happening, just abstain for a while and let the tension build up. Husband and I touch, kiss, hug, and squeeze—but we don't go all the way all the time. It's a two-way tease, but we both know what it will lead to. Finally, we pounce on each other, and go at it like a couple of teenagers! It almost feels like the first time! You do appreciate it.

Once you've committed to a relationship don't take sex for granted, as if that part of your life doesn't have to be tended to. It has to be taken care of just like your financial life, your spiritual life, your health, your career, and your family.

You may go through those periods that I call "dry times," when you don't have sex. Well, it ain't up to anyone but you to decide when you need to have sex and how many times.

How often have you seen Dr. Ruth on TV and wondered when and in what position she does it? Or is she all talk? My imagination can't stretch that far.

I think some of the "experts" aren't getting any sex because they're so intense about it, so uptight about it. Maybe the reason they write about it is because they don't get none.

To me all those sex books are a waste of time. Explore yourself and explore your partner. Your partner should do the same. You should be in tune with each other. Take all the time you need, because if this is a forever relationship or marriage, you got a whole lot of time!

And of course part of the discovery process is exploring yourself. You can have great sex with yourself. It's healthy, normal, and a very good way of getting in touch with yourself. If you can't make yourself feel good how can you tell him how to make you feel good? Sometimes nothing is better for you than you, and what better way to practice safe sex?

SEXUAL POTHOLES

I love sleeping naked so that I can just take in all my husband's body heat. But thanks to the earthquakes in California, Husband sleeps in pajamas and makes me sleep with shoes by the bed and with my nightgown on, because he doesn't want me running through the house and out the door naked if the "big one" hits.

We always used to sleep bare-naked, even during Cleveland winters that are so cold you have to put plastic over the windows. The whole house was weatherproofed and the only thing I slept in were socks and the only thing he slept in was me!

Girlfriend, when the big Northridge earthquake hit on January 17, 1994, I was sleeping butt-naked. Husband jumps out of the bed, hears all the glass breaking, and from that time on I haven't been allowed to sleep naked. If we make love at bedtime, afterwards he puts on his pajamas and tells me to put on my nightgown.

> Me: "But I'm goin' to sleep!"
> Husband: "Put it on!"
> Me: "Aw, do I gotta?"
> Husband: "Yes! You never know when the big one is going to hit!"
> Me: "I thought the big one just did. . . ."
> Husband: "Very funny. Now put that gown on. You ain't gonna be runnin' through here while the house falls down on us and then have them dig you out while you're naked. None of this Marilyn Monroe dying-naked stuff—so put on your gown."

♥

99

♥

And Husband will not turn out the lights until that night-gown is on. He has the "earthquake sex syndrome"—and with all those aftershocks I'm afraid there's no cure.

WHAT IF HE'S GREAT AND THE SEX ISN'T?

So what do you do when he's thoughtful, kind, has a great job, helps around the house, is always there for the kids, and showers you with surprise gifts, but he's lacking in the sex department? This is a solid, good-guy type of Biscuit Head. He likes to kick back and watch TV to relax. He's easygoing and happy with the simple things in life. Sex to him may mean some kissing, rolling over on top of you, doing it, and then quickly getting up and going into the bathroom. Doesn't sound too good to Mother Love.

I got a Girlfriend whose husband makes love to her quickly in the morning and then says, "I gotta go!"—meaning he has to get to work. Now, she's left with her legs wide open, still in the foreplay stage, and he's on his way out the door. This is where masturbation comes in handy, because if you don't release that sexual energy that's been building up, you're just going to be in an agitated state for the rest of the day. At times like this I've got to think about Mother and her vibrator theory.

Masturbation is not the nasty, disgusting thing you think or you've been told. Shoot, what's more nasty: you finishing where Husband or Boyfriend left off or you raisin' hell with everyone you come in contact with for the rest of the day? Girlfriend, you know how aggravated you can feel when you're almost there, when he is already there but leaves you hangin'.

If you really like this Biscuit Head, but he doesn't know what he's doing when it comes to sex, take your time and show him what needs to be done. Take it slowly because he may be extremely shy, or, believe it or not, he may be inexperienced. Not all men are out there porkin' everything that's movin' with a skirt on.

Just remember, Girlfriend, like anything else, the more you practice the better you get. Also try what I call alternative sex. This means giving him a back rub with some nice lotion. Or a foot massage or pedicure. The point is to touch him as much as you can in nonsexual ways and he will relax. Massage him, stroke him—and take note of the areas that seem more sensitive.

And, Girlfriend, strut your stuff butt-naked. The more relaxed you are, the more relaxed he'll become.

If a man is really good, but the sex isn't, he should be willing to learn. If not, there could be a problem that has nothing to do with you. And that means it ain't gonna make no difference what you do.

You could sit on top of the TV with your legs open, smelling kissing soft, but this will accomplish nothing because somewhere in his sex life he became psychologically scarred. If this is the case, it may turn out that he's too rough when you do make love, maybe even to the point of abuse. And makin' love ain't about all that. I'd be worried.

If he is a nice person, but the sex is violent or angry, that's a problem you want to get away from. This is the "riffraff" we talked about before.

But if this ain't the case, take your time with him. Don't be surprised if he asks you if you've had several lovers. Tell him, "No, a few thorough lovers, and I want to share with you everything I know so that we both feel good."

If you keep stroking his ego along with his wanker, it will eventually all come together.

If Boyfriend is a cold fish and isn't willing to try to change, move on. Why stay attached to so much frustration? Good sex happens when both of you meet in the middle: he gives you what you want and you give him what he wants. And you experiment!

It really all comes down to what works for you. If you're satisfied with what you have, hey! Work with it, Girlfriend. Now, I gotta have real good sex. This is what works for me, and fortunately for Biscuit Head Husband.

Put in the effort if you think he's worth it. If not: NEXT!

TO SEX, OR NOT TO SEX

You're dog tried or he's dog tired. Or maybe sex isn't the main course at the moment. This is a good time to be

affectionate. Try lots of hugging and kissing. Health reasons may prevent lovemaking, but that doesn't mean you
can't be affectionate.

This gets back to the importance of being in tune with
one another's bodies. Especially your menstrual cycle,
which can really affect your sex life.

Do you suffer from PMS? Buy Husband or Boyfriend
a book that explains why your hormones are out of whack,
causing your mood swings. Explain to him how you feel
physically, mentally, and emotionally.

I remember Husband telling my son about my hormones. My son was about seven when he became aware of
my bizarre monthly behavior.

One day I had a royal fit on them. I had fixed this
really fancy, elaborate meal. I had roasted a chicken, made
dressing, macaroni and cheese, and corn bread and collard
greens and cabbage, and a pound cake and corn soufflé—I
was off into it!

102

> Son: "You know, Daddy, we could of went to
> McDonald's and she wouldn't have to
> cook all this. . . ."
> Husband: "Oh, yeah—that would have been
> easier, huh?"
> Me: "Easy? *Fine!* Y'all ain't gotta even eat this!"

Girlfriend, I flipped everything off the table and onto the
floor. I got a bad habit of doing this when I get mad—I
was just so agitated!

> Husband: "Oh God, I forgot. . . ."
> Me: "I stood up here all day to cook this really
> fine meal and I'm bleeding like a hog, I

got cramps. Well, you-all ain't never got
to eat what I cook again!" (Yeah, I started
cryin'. . . .)

Son: "Well, Daddy, what's wrong with
   Mommy? Why she screamin' and hollerin'
   like that? Why she flip all the food off
   the table 'cause we said we wanted to eat
   at McDonald's and didn't want to eat this
   big fancy meal she fixed for us? What is
   she talkin' about when she says she's
   bleeding like a hog? What do that mean?"

Husband: "Oh, I'm so sorry. . . . Please forgive
   me."

103

Well, I was just whoopin' and hollerin' and screamin' and
cryin' as I ran through the house. Husband got me to lie
down. I could hear him explaining to our son about how I
couldn't help myself and that it was a female thing that all
big girls go through once a month with their bodies.

Son: "This gonna come every month?"
Husband: "Yeah, until she gets to be old."
Son: "Well, ain't she already old?"
Husband: "Not old enough—this is going to
   be going on for a long time."
Son: "Well, what do I have to do?"
Husband: "Son, just stay out of her way."

I started laughing as I heard them cleaning up the mess and
Husband trying to explain to Son just exactly how old "old"
is. As our son got older we taught him more about women's
bodies and how he had to be sensitive to their feelings
during "their time of the month."

LET'S WRAP IT UP!

There was a period in my life when Husband and I were just so busy. We were remodeling the house. I was sanding and stripping the woodwork while Husband was building the floors and putting the cold-water line in. On top of all of this, we were both holding down jobs and raising our son. Our sex life had vanished somewhere in all the sawdust.

I really needed some physical attention from my man, but everything was so hit-and-miss; I'd be climbing into bed and he'd be gettin' up. Passing strangers.

I wanted to be touched and sucked and licked and kissed all over. I needed my chocolate lollipop, but Husband was so into what he was doing that I think he forgot about old Mr. Wanker.

I decided to plan a romantic evening just for the two of us. An evening when I'd just be his woman and he'd just be my man. I called up my sister and had to pay her twenty-five dollars (that cow!) to watch our son for the weekend. And I called all of our friends and told them not to call us after 8:30 because our special evening was starting at 9:00—this was going to be our time alone.

I went to the open-air market and hand-picked the biggest, freshest strawberries I could find. We were still eating meat in those days, so I went to the butcher and had him cut two of the prettiest porterhouse steaks you've ever seen in your life.

I came home and cleaned the house spic-and-span, put new sheets on our bed. I had candles burning all through the house: it was lookin' and smellin' so fine that I wanted to just go ahead and start without him.

My salad was perfect.

My potatoes were perfect.

Husband likes strawberry shortcake, so I had sliced strawberries over the cake I had made from scratch. Shoot, I even made my own whipped cream!

Oh, I was so excited, because he was going to come in that door and come up the stairs (we lived on the second floor of a duplex), and then I would have my dramatic moment as he took me, wrapped in Saran Wrap, in his arms—wrapped in Saran Wrap?

Okay. One of those sex books talked about meeting your man at the door in Saran Wrap. (I told you I was desperate.) I had oiled my entire body and wrapped myself in clear plastic—yeah, it took two boxes.

My hair was perfect, my makeup was just right, painted fingernails and toe dots. I was ready for everything and anything Husband wanted to do!

Here was my plan: I would run a hot bath for him and after dinner I would take off his clothes and bathe him in the soothing, lightly scented water. After I bathed him I was going to dry him with a big, fluffy towel and wrap him in a red terry-cloth bathrobe, still warm from the dryer.

Girlfriend, I was going to lotion his body down and I had put baby powder all over the sheets. We were going to have strawberries, champagne, and *moi* for dessert!

Okay?

I had done everything those sex books said. It was perfect!

Girlfriend, Husband comes up the steps and I turn on the light so he can see me glowing in my Saran Wrap sarong.

Wrong.

First thing he notices are the candles burning.

Husband: "Did you forget to pay the light
 bill? Why are you burning all these
 candles? And what have you done by
 wrapping yourself up with the stuff you
 put over the bowls in the refrigerator?
 Now, how you gonna wrap the food up?
 Girl, you better put some clothes on—
 it's cold up in here! What's wrong with
 you? Why are all the lights off? You
 know I don't like eating late like this.
 Why you fixin' such a big, heavy meal
 like this?"

Me: "You're going to sit down and enjoy this
 sexy moment, even if it kills you!"

Husband: "I want you to put the lights on
 and blow out those candles because
 you're gonna walk past them in your
 plastic wrap and set yourself on fire!
 Now, this ain't a smart thing to do—see,
 you been reading too many of those
 books!"

I was devastated. I told him he could take his own damn
clothes off and give himself a bath. Well, he went and got
on the phone. I went into the bathroom and unwrapped
myself, took a bath, and washed off the oil, put on my old
nightgown, and got into bed. I could hear him taking his
bath in my bathwater.

Now I had forgotten about the champagne and strawberries. Husband comes in and I'm thinkin' everything will
be all right. I turn on the music and bring out the strawberries that I had dipped in chocolate, which I had melted
in the double boiler, and powdered sugar.

> Husband: "Now why is you eatin' stuff that
> sweet at this late of an hour? You're
> gonna get a cavity. And you're drinkin'
> with those berries? Girl, you're gonna
> throw up!"
>
> Me: "Shut up! Shut up! Shut up! I have gone
> through a great deal of effort to make
> you a romantic evening like they have in
> those sex books and I'm not going to let
> you spoil my mood, so just take your
> robe off and let's just do it and get it over
> with!"

I could have cared less if he was satisfied. I just took care
of myself as if he were my boy toy. He would never have
another romantic moment like this again—and if he did, it
would not be for such a long time that he would have no
choice but to appreciate it.

Of course Biscuit Head thought that I had totally
overreacted to the whole thing. Now, he thought this was
so funny that he started telling one of his friends.

> Friend: "Damn! She did all that? Man, I would
> kill just to come home to a clean house. I
> don't think you realize what kind of
> woman you've got."
>
> Husband: "But I want my bowls wrapped in
> Saran Wrap—not her buns!"

His friend continued telling him what a jewel I was. But
Biscuit Head always took me for granted and always
thought that this was the kind of stuff I should do for him
anyway. He was entitled to this because he was king and

he was running the show. What I had done was part of my "wifely, womanly duty." I had just gotten a little too carried away this time.

For me, this wasn't what was happenin'. Now, he didn't miss it until he didn't have it. You can't appreciate your water until your well runs dry.

Well, his well ran dry. . . . He was sorry, begged for forgiveness.

I was the Nefertiti of Naughtiness!

The Sex Goddess of the Universe.

And Biscuit Head was nothing more than the King of Crap.

💜   💜   💜   💜

108

💜

Yeah, after this he learned to appreciate our romantic moments, regardless of the theme. Now he's really into it. We have a net that we drape over our bed, like a mosquito net, and I receive him in my boudoir.

Sex is special.

Sex is personal.

Sex is sacred when it's an extension of your love.

Sex allows us time to connect with one another. At the moment of orgasm it is as if God has taken a deep breath and held it so that time stops.

Sex is your "time out" from the wear and tear of everyday life. And an orgasm is an incredible pause in time.

I can give you endless suggestions, share tips that I've tried and Girlfriend has tried, but only you will know what works for you. Nobody, and I mean nobody, can tell you how to have a better sex life because sexuality is so individualistic.

Whether it's Dr. Ruth or my mother, they can suggest but cannot tell me or you what will excite, stimulate, and turn us on. This is why you must become your own sex expert—and, Girlfriend, it's worth your time.

I know what works for us. And all I can do is share with you what works for me and Husband as I urge you to experiment and explore.

Intimacy is wonderful.

Mother, do you hear me?

After twenty-three years of marriage we still clean up real fine.

Mother love ©

CHAPTER SEVEN

We're very married—now what?
—All You Married Folks

♥   ♥   ♥

*M*y husband is my first and only husband of twenty-three years. Being married more than once would just get on my last working nerves. But if it takes more than one husband for you, Girlfriend, then that's what it takes for you.

I'm a strong believer in really getting to know who you are going to share your life with before you take the big plunge. Sometimes when you think you know someone, you don't because people can put up these really good fronts. But eventually they will get to a place where they will change. You can only hope that it's for the better and not for the worse.

And these dunderheads can be so fickle. There's a reason it took Husband and me thirteen years to say "I do." We both wanted to be sure.

When the preacher, rabbi, minister, pastor, or whoever said to you, "For better or for worse," he or she wasn't kidding. And if you don't work as a team from the "get-go," your marriage is not going to work. I haven't met one person who's been married for twenty minutes who has said that marriage is easy.

Most of us Girlfriends have this fantasy that the courtship that leads to marriage will continue with its flowers, kisses, and sweetness. No, you've just barely got started. Marriage is complicated, confusing, sometimes crazy, and requires a tremendous amount of patience and compromise from both of you.

Yeah, you're gonna go through good times and bad times, but, baby, just stick with it and ride the rough times out if you can. Regardless of what's going on between the two of you, somewhere in the back of your mind remember that marriage is an honor and a privilege. You made promises. You took vows. And it will probably take you your whole married life for you to figure one another out.

PUT UP YOUR DUKES!

When Husband was still Boyfriend, and we were first together, I felt very insecure because he had numerous friends and people just really enjoyed being around him. Especially women. I think my feelings were normal. Aren't most of us in love afraid of losing our man?

Before Boyfriend would leave to go on a business trip he'd say, "Here's the money, here's the credit cards, here's the bank cards, here's the keys to my car"—kiss—"See you, I'm going to New York."

> Me: "Why can't I go to New York?"
> Boyfriend: "Well, it's business and it's just a
>   bunch of guys going."

112

Me: "Well, why do a bunch of men have to go
    to New York?"

So I'm having a fit while he's kissing me and giving me a
stack of money. And I scream, "See, that's your way to solve
everything! Just throw money at me! I don't want your
money!"

Well, of course I would take it and spend it and run
up his credit cards and not think about all the gas I used
up as I drove his car. I had the right. He was always going
to New York City or Washington to do business or visit
his fraternity brothers. And he would never take me with
him. Here I was, lost in Ohio.

During one of his trips, when we were living in our
first little apartment, I tore that sucker up! I got so mad that
I knocked over plants, slapped dishes off the sink, threw
food out of the cupboards and onto the floor, snatched all
of his clothes out of the closet, threw his underwear ev-
eryplace, and dumped dishwashing liquid over everything.
In my hissy fit I had created the worst possible mess. Enter
Boyfriend right after I'd thrown the TV on the floor. I was
a madwoman!

Girlfriend, he came into the house and looked around
at what I had done. I'm sitting on the edge of the bed,
having just finished my rage and still panting. I'm sure he
was thinkin', Oh, now she's gone and went crazy on me.

Boyfriend looks around and says, "You know, you've
made a mess out here."

"Hell, yeah, I made a mess! You don't wanna take no
time to spend with me. You just wanna run around with
your sorry-ass friends and big-head-ass women—oh! But
you want me to run the vacuum cleaner cook our meals
iron your shirts make our bed and let you "have some"

♥

113

♥

whenever you feel like it—oh! But I can't wanna go no-place!"

By this time I am standing up in the middle of the bed in an entire sweat. My hair has napped up so bad that it looks like someone plucked it off my head, balled it up, and threw it back to Africa before putting it back on my head. I'm still rantin' and ravin' in my hissy fit while he slowly takes a letter opener from the dresser and starts cleaning his fingernails.

My hissy scream, "ARE YOU LISTENIN' TO ME?"

"Yeah, I'm listenin' to you." And he would just look at me.

"HOW CAN YOU SAY YOU LOVE ME AND TREAT ME LIKE THIS?"

"But I do love you."

"NO YOU DON'T!"

When I paused he asked, "Are you finished?"

"HELL NO, I AIN'T FINISHED! AND LET ME TELL YOU ABOUT BLAH BLAH BLAH BLAH BLAH BLAH BLAH BLAH, and, BLAH, BLAH, BLAH!"

"Well, are you finished?"

"NO!" And I would go off for another fifteen minutes.

"Are you finished?"

Finally, "Yes, I'm finished."

Boyfriend got out of his chair, walked over to our bed, took me off the bed, and made me sit on the edge of the bed, real calm, real peaceful—kind of like a psychiatrist, ya know. Goes into the bathroom to get a wet towel to cool me off because I'm sweating like a hog by now. He lays me down and puts the towel on my head as he says, "You need to take a nap. Rest yourself because I know that took a lot out of you and you have such a mess to clean up. So take your time. Get up when you feel like it and then you can take care of the mess. . . ."

I was so outdone by his calm behavior that I just couldn't believe it. I mean, he had just cracked my face in fifteen different places. Here I'm havin' the fit of all fits, where most men would be saying, "Bitch, shut up!" But Boy-friend was so calm, letting me get all my stuff out, and he still acts that way today. When I'm havin' a fit or jumpin' up and down about something, he'll say, "Feel better now?" And I'll answer, "Yes, I feel better now."

After this episode I never tore up my home again. I got up and it took me four hours to make that tiny apartment right. I'm a quick study. I only had to tear up my house once to realize I didn't need to do it again. I told Boyfriend, "Okay, we ain't never gonna be doin' this crap no more. If we break stuff it's going to be stuff we don't care about, but I don't want the cleanup."

Girlfriend, no matter how much you love one another, you are going to have fights after you're married just like you did before you were married. They're normal, natural, and it's much better to share your feelings, even if it means yelling, than to pretend that nothing is bothering you when it is. But don't take this to the extreme like I did, and there is no reason you have to fight every day. Sure, you should discuss and express your point of view. We all have our own beliefs and needs. And we all need to be heard. This is why compromise is so important.

> Me: "I need more affection right now. I don't
>   like it when you don't give me any."
> Husband: "I'm not a huggy, kissy type of
>   person."

Husband and I could have allowed this to become a prob-lem in our relationship or we could compromise. We chose

115

to compromise because this was important to me, and Husband wanted me to feel more comfortable. When you compromise it means that there is something in your life that you feel is significant enough to work at and improve.

When approaching a problem in your marriage, before you explode, consider the following questions:

• Is this important enough for us to work on?

• Is it important enough to make the necessary changes in our relationship to make things okay?

• Or is it not worth fussing about because it will only hurt our relationship?

Showing affection is hard for Husband, but he loves me so much and he wants to make me happy, so we work on it together and every day it gets better. We work at making each other happy. I try not to be too demanding and he hugs and kisses me more often. Sometimes he'll just take me in his arms and hold me.

This is the best.

No words are spoken. (Yeah, I know when to shut up!)

He just holds me.

Do we fight? Of course, although I must say my diplomatic skills have definitely improved through the years.

Like most Girlfriends, I was not always so wise. When I was younger I used to make wild scenes in public, cussing and swearing like a drunken sailor.

One time Boyfriend (he wasn't Husband yet) had taken all the money out of our bank account to use for one of these "get-rich-quick" schemes without telling me. He didn't tell me because he was sure he would get the money back into the account before I found out. Well, I went to the bank on Monday morning and found out that our $3,000 account had $15 in it. I was not mad because the money was gone. I was mad because he didn't tell me.

> Boyfriend: "Well, if I told you about it, you
> would have said, 'No, you ain't taking no
> money out of the bank. That money is
> for our household and our baby!' "

Girlfriend, with my baby boy on my hip, standing in front of the Bank of America, I cussed my man out—up one side and down the other—from an amazing grace to a floating opportunity.

We had a big crowd gathering around us. I said and did everything but actually slap him.

> Me: "I don't know what the hell you think, but
> when I get home all your stuff better be
> gone—matter of fact, take everything you
> bought!"

This was a really stupid way for me to behave. And on top of my crazy behavior, we have a little bit of a problem: I've bought everything. To this day Husband hasn't even bought his own underwear since he was nineteen years old.

Things have changed over the years. Now I am not afraid of my husband, nor do I in any way feel threatened by him. I respect him because he is my husband and the head of our house. This is why I no longer ridicule or fight with him in public. If I've got something to say about him,

117

he will be very right about "whatever" until we get into our house and close the door. And then I start.

> Me: "Your ass was wrong, you know you was
> wrong, and when we go back you better
> tell them! I don't care how you do it, but
> I was right and you gotta fix it!"
> Husband (sometimes): "Okay. Next time I'll fix
> it."

Enough said. He respects my feelings and listens to what I say because I don't humiliate him in public, and because I only bring it up once. I may rant, rave, hiss, and scream until I've worked up a sweat and my drawers are wet, *but I don't belabor my point.* This is not always an easy thing to do, and I may have to swallow my tongue or bite my lip, but it is the most effective way to handle and end a fight.

SPOIL YOUR MATE

Enough with the fighting. Let's spread a little joy, Girl-friend! From the moment you say "I do," start spoiling your mate. I don't care how aggravated you feel or how tough your day has been, do something extra special to spoil your mate every day. This makes you indispensable and even more irresistible than you already are. Spoiling your mate perpetuates the magic we all enjoyed during the courtship. And it certainly makes his day nicer.

In fact, Husband and I make it a practice to do some-thing special for one another each day. Maybe he'll fold the laundry for me or clean up the kitchen. I'll be out shop-ping and see a shirt that I know he has to have. I'll buy his favorite cookies. He'll bring home a little bouquet of flowers. Or he'll mail me a card of affection during his lunch break.

Husband loves breakfast in bed and he gets it at least once a week. I love a quiet bath and knowing nothing is expected of me afterwards so that I can really relax. Both Husband and Son respect this. We're all spoiled a little bit every day and it sure feels good. If you can't think of anything special, why not just give Husband a simple kiss, look into his eyes, and tell him how much you appreciate all that he does for you.

And even if you're having a "dumb day," you've got to do something nice to spoil him. It'll make your dumb day a whole lot better.

Most important of all is to spoil him without expecting anything in return. It shows generosity of spirit that comes straight from your heart. You can be miserable, but it will make you feel just a little bit better to know that you added something positive to Husband's day.

No matter what, every day:

I treat Husband like a king. I do it to please him.

And guess what?

He treats me like a queen. He does it to please me.

YOUR HOME IS WHERE YOUR MARRIAGE LIVES

Your home is your castle.

Your home is your sanctuary.

Your home is where your marriage lives.

As much as it needs to be organized and clean, your home also needs to be fun. How do you put fun into your everyday space? Spice it up! Give it new energy. This means rearranging furniture and replacing the tired old towels,

♥

119

♥

sheets, tablecloth, and kitchen curtains with something new. The littlest changes can make the biggest difference— and for very little money. Mother taught me this.

In fact, my mother was a decorating freak with the attention span of a sixteen-year-old when it came to household furnishings. She would go through all six rooms of our house, give away all the furniture, and buy all new stuff. Where did she get the money? Besides always having a job, it beats me. That was a question we never asked, and she always found a way. I remember times when, out of the blue, she'd make the announcement:

"Clean out the bedrooms! Clean out the bedrooms! New furniture is coming!"

Us: "Well, when is it coming?"
Mother: "It's walking down the walkway right
        now!"
Us: "What? What? What?"

There would be new beds and new dressers for each of us. And she would change the color scheme of the house every season. We had a winter house, a spring house, a summer house, and a fall house. Walls and ceilings would be painted to match the seasons.

Mother hired her very creative, drug-addict brother to do the painting. What he did was outrageous because he was always high when he did it. But his creations were fun! Why, one summer we had a red kitchen ceiling and orange swinging doors going into the kitchen.

This tradition lives on in my home. (No, I don't paint my ceilings red and my doors aren't orange.) Redecorating is fun to do, doesn't have to be expensive, and seems to give my whole family a burst of energy and a better attitude. Yes, I do change the house around, but not to the extreme that Mother did. And I do one room at a time, where Mother would go full tilt!

A new comforter, adding more pillows on the bed, and different throw rugs on our bedroom floor perks up our sex life. And there's something special about sleeping on new sheets, bathing with scented soap, and drying your booty, big or small, with new, fluffy towels.

KEEP YOUR DEEP DISCUSSIONS OUT OF THE BEDROOM

Your job is what you get paid for, your life is what you do. There's nothing wrong with talking about your day, but most people should keep those arguments out of the bedroom.

Whatever it is that you do or say, make sure that you can lie down and go to sleep with it. If you have tried everything you can do, said everything that you can say, lived that day in a positive way, then you can lie down and go to sleep and you ain't got nothin' to worry about.

Don't take conversation to bed, unless it's something fun or some sex talk. Give one another fifteen minutes at the end of the day to share what's happened. And think very carefully about where you're gonna have a fight about bills and money.

I know a Girlfriend who discusses business and money matters only in one room: the kitchen. She and Husband have agreed that this is their spot. Here, all of the emotion, tension, frustration, and worry can be aired out. The agreement is that when they leave the kitchen the discussion is over.

But now I gotta eat crow because Husband and I are

an exception to the rule. We do just the opposite of what I have advised. We do our best conferring about what we're gonna do with our lives and our finances in the bedroom because it works for us. Why? I don't really know. Maybe it's because in the bedroom we feel like we're on an equal level.

Again, you gotta do what works for you as a couple. I've heard people say that you should never discuss sexual issues while you're having sex; well, when are you supposed to talk about them? When you're driving down the street? When you're shopping? Might as well share your information with the cashier. When it comes to sexual issues, discuss it while it's happening.

Before you discuss, open up your mouth, think about what you're going to say, when you're going to say it, and the best way to say it so hopefully you can avoid arguing. Sometimes the simplest things can turn into a full-blown argument because you haven't thought through what you're going to say. An example:

If you don't like pasta, and he keeps making pasta, you are going to have to figure out a nice way to tell him.

"Honey, we've had a lot of pasta lately. How about something different? I appreciate your effort, but I just don't like pasta. I'd love some fresh fish for dinner—maybe with some rice and vegetables? What do you think?"

Now, how can he get mad at you when you approach the problem like that?

HELPING ONE ANOTHER KICK BAD HABITS

Bad habits are personal, so I'll just tell you about one of mine.

I chose to be a smoker.

I choose to be a nonsmoker.

While kicking the habit, every day I told myself, "No, I choose not to smoke." That first week I was a bitch on wheels. It was so hard I was biting metal.

> Husband to Son: "Just stay away from your
>   mama right now because she's really
>   acting like a bitch. . . ."
> Me: "Oh! I'm trying to quit and now you're
>   calling me a bitch!"
> Husband: "Baby, I don't think you're a bitch—
>   you're just acting like one right now. I
>   know this is a real hard time we're going
>   through but this too shall pass. . . ."

123

I'd get all fired up. "Get away from me! I hate your Black butt! Just get away from me! I don't wanna talk to y'all! I hate y'all. . . ."

Then I'd break down and cry. "I just can't quit . . . but I don't wanna be a smoker. . . . I don't wanna die. . . . Oh, please help me, help me, help me, help me. . . ."

> Husband: "I'll help you, baby. Don't worry."
> Me: "You don't love me. You don't care nothin'
>   about me. You just think I'm fat and
>   smoke."
> Husband: "Well, you are fat and you do
>   smoke, but I love you anyway. So what's
>   your point? See, now, I'm glad you're
>   comin' off cigarettes. . . ." Husband turns
>   to Son: "Can you imagine her comin' off
>   of drugs? We'd have to shoot her."

Oh, me quittin' smoking was bad. It was *bad*. I didn't wanna cook so I was slappin' dishes off the table. If they said the wrong thing to me I was liable to do anything. One day I stood before the two of 'em and just screamed my head off.

After a week of no smoking, one morning I got up to fix Husband breakfast in bed (this is some of that spoiling I was talking about). My son came in and we were all sitting in our bed having pancakes and syrup. I was sincerely trying to make up for being so hateful. I was trying to be nice.

As you know, I change my bedroom four or five times a year. The current boudoir theme was an elegant, majestic purple comforter and emerald green rugs on the floor. Girlfriend, all my husband said was, "Can you get us some more hot syrup?"

I blew. "Hell, no! I ain't gettin' no more syrup!" *Splat!* I slapped all the food onto the middle of our beautiful bed. He looked at me quietly and said, "You know, it's going to be awfully hard to get all of the syrup off of this bed."

"Excuse me? I am having a fit! Why are you concerned about the comforter?"

Staying calm is his MO.

But isn't this true of most dunderhead men?

They're being cool while we be havin' our hissy fits, sweatin' in our drawers!

Yeah, I got through it and did kick the habit. And I have to thank my patient, understanding husband for helping me.

DON'T BE A SPORTS WIDOW

It can happen in any marriage: the television goes on and Husband tunes you out as he tunes into the sports channel.

You might as well not exist, because that home run, point, touchdown, or fumble is all your Biscuit Head sees.

My mother loved football, so from a very early age I learned all about it. By the time I was ten I knew about tight ends and wide receivers. (By the time I was fifteen tight ends and wide receivers had taken on a whole new meaning!) I knew what they meant when they said, "Third down, four to go." Men loved my sports knowledge and I became a "guy chick." Shoot, I could whoop and holler with the best of them, and I knew exactly what I was getting excited about.

Girlfriend, whether you like it or not, sports are a big part of most men's lives. But you don't have to be a sports widow. You can participate in the game.

125

The best way to begin is to start reading the sports page of the newspaper. First pick one sport that you like and then choose a team. I've got Girlfriends who choose their favorite team by how many good-looking guys are on it.

Some choose by the shape of the ball that goes with the sport. What excites you more? Seeing a round ball slip through a hoop, an almond-shaped ball fly through the air and over a bar, or a small, hard ball hit with a bat that makes it fly way out there somewhere?

Husband loves basketball because of the rapid pace and contact. Girlfriend, I like it because the players are a bunch of long, strong, tall men running and sweating. Damn! They have to be great lovers because of their endurance. And those butts and thighs—what a picnic we could have!

Girlfriend, whether or not you can get interested in a sport doesn't really matter if you know how to make the best of halftime. Ten minutes before halftime I run a hot bubble bath for Husband, fix him a tray of cheese, crackers, fruit, and an ice-cold beer, put on a sexy nightgown, undress Husband, and put him into the tub. As he lies back and sips his cold beer I bathe him. Of course I always bring our miniature TV into the bathroom so that if he's not done bathing we can continue to watch the game.

Halftime is only about fifteen minutes long. If Husband tries to touch me in any of those "special places" or is even thinkin' about doin' the wild thing, I tell him we have to watch the rest of the game first! And I'm as eager as he is about seeing which team wins. After these memorable halftimes, including our personal postgame wrap-up, Husband always says, "All the guys should get to enjoy sports this way—you should write a book!"

Recently Husband and I talked about taking up golf. It's a sport that we could do together. But we're both afraid we'd be bored. And I don't know about wearing those funky golf clothes, those bright plaid pants and color-coordinated shirts.

Now, I have a Girlfriend whose husband is a golf fanatic. He plays every Saturday and almost every Sunday. She doesn't get it, can't stand to play it, and thinks trying to hit a little ball across grass and sand and into a little hole marked with a flag is ridiculous.

But here's a smart Girlfriend. Since she wants to be with her man, she drives the golf cart and cleans his balls in those little gizmos that you jerk up and down and up and down with your hand. Yep, different strokes for different folks. I'm not sure if Husband and I are ready for this one yet.

126

IF YOU THINK HE'S CHEATING ON YOU OR YOU'RE THINKIN' OF CHEATING ON HIM

Girlfriend, we all know that two wrongs don't make a right—this is so bogus. What an easy out! To cheat is not good. I have nothing positive to say about this kind of situation.

You made a vow, you took an oath to marry this person, to spend your life with him. I told you from the beginning this was not going to be easy. Doesn't your word mean anything to anyone—especially you? Where's your self-respect?

So you're bored with Husband.

You think the grass is greener somewhere else? If your grass is brown it's because you haven't been watering it, tending to it. So of course the grass is gonna seem greener somewhere else. But how do you know it's real grass? It might be AstroTurf!

Cheating is another excuse for laziness. When you've been with someone for a considerable amount of time, you've got to be on your toes to keep the relationship alive.

I think one of the reasons a person cheats is because they want to be around somebody who doesn't know them as well as the person they're cheating on. They don't have to be as honest or as real with a lover; it's like living in a fantasy. They don't have to face the music.

Hello, fantasy world! No laundry, cookin', or cleanin'—just sex and lots of thick, sweet talk! A lover will treat you special and you'll get to do all this romantic stuff, including sneaking around.

When you love somebody you don't go sneakin'

127

around with a lover—and I don't care what the magazines say. If you don't want to be committed to your marriage in every way, then end that relationship. Allow it to end or make it end.

I think it's ridiculous when a Girlfriend says to me, "Oh, she just took my man away from me!"

Ain't nobody gonna take anyone away from you. If your man leaves you, or you leave him, it's a conscious choice of the person who is walking out. Nobody is making anyone do this. Just like it's a conscious choice to stay together and work on the marriage together.

The problem is that we are all looking for instant gratification. We want everything to be perfect all the time: how we look, how we feel, how we talk, how we act.

Wait a minute!

What happened to the reality of this thing?

How come we can't find joy in each other, regardless of the situation? I have a story to tell you:

When I knew that Boyfriend and I were going to get married, that it was a forever kind of thing—or at least for as long as we could stand each other—one day we were lying in bed and doin' "the wild thing." Oh, we were just clappin', and slammin', and whoppin' and whappin' and it was raining really hard. I had called a man earlier in the day to find out the cost of putting new gutters on our house. As we moaned and groaned in our pleasure, we could hear the rain sloshing through the gutters. It sounded like the whole house was just going to float away.

As we continued making love to the beat of the thunder and the lightning, I suddenly said, "Know what, honey? Gutter man called back and said he'll be here tomorrow. He's going to give us an estimate. . . ."

Husband (still in motion): "Oh, crap! What's
    the estimate on the gutters gonna be? Oh
    well, guess we gotta have them. . . ."
Me (still in motion): "Yeah, we need new
    gutters."

What a conversation to have suddenly when you're doin'
the wild thing! We were worried about the new gutters but
we didn't miss a beat as we kept makin' love.

If this scenario had happened with someone insecure,
it would have ruined the mood. But for us, because we are
so much in tune with one another, we just continued on
and on.

Personally, after all these years, I think I can safely
say today that I would never be able to love anybody else
like I love Husband. I wouldn't want to cheat on Husband
because I wouldn't want anyone to know my deep, dark
secrets like Husband does.

I don't want another man to know where he can kiss me
and lick me to make me tingle. I don't want another man to
know about any health problems I have. I don't want any
other man to know that I suffer terribly from PMS and what
a witch I can be when I have it. I don't want another man to
know my cooking secrets, or about my hair, whether it's a
hair weave, my hair, or a wig hat. I don't want another man
to know my true bra size and that I like walking around the
house naked when it's just the two of us.

I think my husband feels the same way about all of
his personal things. He doesn't want another woman to
know his angry side, or how I can look at him a certain
way and make him just put a big old smile on his face. I
can be standing next to one of the most gorgeous women

129

in the world and my husband still likes me the best. Sure, he thinks she's beautiful. But I'm his woman!

And then there's the time you put in when you cheat. Think about it. you gotta break in new sex habits, lie, figure out a place to meet; you can't leave the house looking too gorgeous; you have find a place to hide your car; and you can't wear the same panties with your husband that you wear with your lover. Cheating on your spouse seems like too much work for me. And I haven't even mentioned the guilt you're gonna feel when you're back home with Husband and he's greeting you with open arms.

What did Mother have to say about cheating? She said, "It's better to be with the dirt you know than the dirt you don't know."

Cheating just creates another problem on top of the original problem that has led you to cheat. Spend that energy working on your marriage instead of jumping through hoops for a couple of hours of fantasy.

And what about your kids?

What if they found out?

I can only imagine the insecurity they would feel. This could ruin their day, their week, their school year—and just about every part of their lives. Kids thrive on security. Take it away and they're likely to react in any way imaginable, depending on their age.

I know I don't sound very "cosmopolitan," but this is how Mother Love feels. There is no definition in any dictionary that says cheating is a good thing. It's not a good thing if you cheat on your income taxes and it's not a good thing if you cheat on your mate.

I can't make this right for you. I can only be your Girlfriend and tell you that cheating is not the thing to do. If you do decide to cheat, one way or another you will pay a price. When you least expect it, it will jump up and slap the taste right out of your mouth. And good luck going to sleep at night with a clear conscience.

HOW TO TELL IF YOUR MARRIAGE IS IN TROUBLE

A few pointers:

You go to the bank and there ain't no money in your joint account.

When the power company turns off your electricity and he hands you a change-of-address card for the post office. Could it be that he's trying to tell you that he doesn't want to live with you anymore? Take the hint, Girlfriend!

When you're washing his laundry, your laundry, and her laundry.

When you got a "wife-in-law." This is the other woman—ya know, the mistress.

When you find out he's got a couple of kids you never knew about who live around the corner . . . and you had been thinkin', Don't all those kids resemble my husband?

When her marriage starts coming to your house.

When his laundry is beginning to look a little sparse—where did all his clothes go? You know he can't be outgrowing them, so he must be leaving them somewhere else.

When he changes his aftershave.

When he's so preoccupied that he's forgotten to feed his dog (who you don't like) for a week. Now that dog is sniffin' around you, probably thinking, Breakfast.

When the dog you raised from a puppy starts barking at you, or he's barkin' more than usual at your Girlfriend, maybe he's trying to tell you something.

When your dog starts sniffin' your husband's crotch.

When you want to do the wild thing and he don't show up!

When everything you look at looks like a phallus and your husband looks like a tadpole.

When you're gettin' yourself all pretty and fancy and you ain't doing it for him.

❤   ❤   ❤

Bottom line? You know your marriage is in trouble when things have changed—and not for the better. What do you do? If he's the one cheating (yeah, I know it really hurts), I'd be direct, open, and honest about it. See how he responds. Does he want to remain married to you? If so, he's going to have to end his affair. Is he willing to go to a marriage counselor with you so that you can both learn what's not working in your relationship?

While you may eventually forgive him, or he will eventually forgive you, this is a period in your marriage that neither one of you will ever forget. But look at yourself in the mirror, Girlfriend, and ask yourself: Is it worth fixing? And if it is, it's gonna be the hardest row you've ever hoed, but you can fix it if it means enough to you.

BOREDOM IS A SORRY EXCUSE FOR LAZINESS

Yeah, sometimes married life gets to be ho-hum. Dumb days are occurring more frequently. Okay, you've got your man; the sex is good and regular; you, he, or both of you have a good job; and your kids have their friends, but you're bored out of your mind.

Boredom is a hard topic for me to talk about because I never get bored. I might get sick of Husband, fantasize about fooling around, think about old boyfriends, but bored? No way! I've never been bored. I'm not sure if I even understand what it really is because it seems impossible to me.

I do believe that boredom is a personal problem that only you can resolve. It's not up to someone else to amuse you. Maybe it's time to focus on what makes you happy.

When I was learning to be my own best friend, I learned that I can still be happy even if I'm alone. As long as I like myself when I look in the mirror, I'm okay. Because if Mother Love isn't all right with herself, how can she help anyone else?

It's so important for you to make sure that you are happy. Because if you are not happy there is no way you can make anyone else happy. Hopefully you entered into marriage with your own individuality, friends, hobbies, activities, etc.

133

Yeah, things do change when you're married because you have another person's feelings to consider and a life to share. In fact, now that you've got another person to be concerned about, and maybe a couple of kids, when do you have time to be bored? I can't imagine. Tell me, please tell Mother Love 'cause she don't get it!

I think boredom is a sorry excuse for laziness. When you give in to it you're telling yourself you're no longer taking responsibility for your life or your actions. Maybe that's how your butt got so big: from sitting and complaining.

When I'm not working (the entertainment industry goes through its dry spells), I'm always doing something because there is always something to do. Here are some questions and suggestions that will help you if you ever find yourself at loose ends:

- Clean out drawers so you'll be able to open any drawer in your house and immediately find whatever you need.

- Clean out the cupboards.

- Arrange and separate your lingerie.

- Better yourself: join an exercise class, or how about a cooking class that will teach you how to cook Chinese?

- Clean out the garbage.

- Throw away those old shoes.

- Clean out your closet.

- Go clean your stove.

- Go clean out your refrigerator.

- Clean out your purse. Now, this has got to be a big job, and just how many pairs of panties are in there?

- Balance your checkbook.

Don't just be sitting there thinking that there is nothing to do. There is always something for you to do. But you just may be too lazy to get up and do it. If this is the case, fess up! You're not bored—you're lazy!

After all of these ideas, tell Mother Love that you're

still bored. I can't think of one human being on this planet who doesn't have something to do. Not one person who can sit in bed and honestly say, "Oh, I'm bored."

How clean is your bathroom floor?

Is there any crud in your tub?

Have the corners in each room been vacuumed?

I have a ten-page list of things to do. Personally, right now I need to:

Clean out my video cabinet.

Sort out my drawers in my drawer! I always need to clean out my underwear drawers because I wear big bloomers.

Find a place to put new clothes because I've dropped two dress sizes and I need to make my seasonal wardrobe change.

Yeah, I have a plethora of chores. And I do certain things every week. This includes: dusting my house, cleaning all the mirrors, vacuuming, doing laundry, mopping floors, sweeping the porch, and changing the beds.

If you've got the time to be bored after all of this, then you must be one hell of a woman. So spend your "free time" helping others. Now, Girlfriend, don't tell me it will take too much of your time—you're bored, remember?

Here are some more suggestions:

• Do something special for yourself, your kids, your man, or even a neighbor.

• Volunteer at the hospital or your church. Take the kids on a nature walk or an urban walk if you live in the city.

• Go to the library and read to the blind.

- Join a charity or start helping with a community project.

- Be an active member in the PTA at your kids' school.

This "helping others" list is endless. So find your niche, connect, and get busy!

❤   ❤   ❤

Girlfriend, if you're still bored, come on over to Mother Love's house because I've got plenty of things for you to do. Honey, we can clean and chitchat.

When I lived in Cleveland, Ohio, Girlfriends and I would get together on the weekends and help each other with housework. It got done twice as fast and we had a good time talkin'. We'd set off bombs for roaches in each house and while the bomb was doing its thing we'd take our kids for haircuts, get our cars washed, do some shopping, then go back and air out the houses, sweep up the roaches, and scrub and clean everything.

As a team we could do two or three houses in one day and still have Girlfriend time. So we didn't get bored. How could we? And we taught our children that there is always plenty for them to do. All they need is some help from you to get started.

> Son: "Mommy, I don't have no nothin' to do."
> Me: "Oh, baby, Mama has plenty of things for
>   you to do. Come on into your room and
>   let's go through your things."

We'd go through his toys, get rid of clothes he'd outgrown, and write letters to relatives. To this day, my eighteen-year-old son never says, "I ain't got nothin' to do," because he knows I'll think of something that has to be done. As Mother always said, Idle hands are the devils workshop!

WHAT TO DO WITH THOSE MEDDLING RELATIVES

When I was growing up in the ghetto you took care of family no matter what. Whether they were alcoholics or heroin addicts or had babies out of wedlock, family was family. And you looked out for one another. These were the only people in the world you could go to who would take you in. This is why it's so important that you make sure, as a part of the head of the family, that your kids and other family members always have a safe place to be. If you grew up in a family where you didn't feel safe, you understand how important this sense of well-being is—especially for your children.

137

If you grew up in an unsafe, unhealthy place, then you know how bitter, how hateful, and how closed-off you can become. You can break the cycle by taking responsibility and not looking back. No, you don't blame the past for the present. You make a conscious effort to make a change, always moving forward in a positive direction.

Unstable relatives are not meddlers, they're just temporarily lost souls who need our help. In fact, it is our obligation to help them get back on their feet so that they can be the best they can be. I've seen some folks beaten down so low that even the simplest acts of kindness begin to change their lives.

Auntie and Uncle (you remember Auntie and her panties) were a couple of drunks. But when they got sober, after we brought them home and dried them out, they were two of the nicest people in the world.

Auntie would make a point, hangover and all, to get up before any one of us and have the house spit clean. She'd cook a big breakfast for us all and make sure our clothes were pressed for school. As long as Auntie and Uncle were living with us they stayed happy and sober. And then on any given day, for no particular reason, she'd say to Mother, "Sister, it's time for us to go. . . ." I missed her, the chatter between her and my mother, but I always knew she'd be back again . . . and she was.

Now, relatives who are meddlers are a whole 'nother story. And I have rules:

> Don't be gettin' in my business.
> Don't be tellin' me about my man.
> Don't tell me how to raise my kid.

Now, I don't mind listening to constructive criticism or intelligent advice. But don't be messin' in my life. My mother's meddling was something I had to deal with because it usually involved money that I needed.

When I got old enough to borrow money from Mother I was known as the hundred-dollar kid because I'd always need at least $100. Mother had a little book to keep track of the money she loaned us—with interest, of course.

> Mother: "Why do you always need at least a
> hundred dollars?"
> Me: "Well shoot, Ma, I gotta keep twenty to
> fifty dollars in my own pocket."

Now, my brothers and sisters never borrowed that kind of money because it was considered "big money."

Me: "Loan me eight hundred dollars."

Mother: "What you need eight hundred dollars for?"

Me: "Do I have to pay it back?"

Mother: "Hell yes, you gotta pay it back with interest!"

Me: "Well, then I don't think it's none of your business what I need it for if I'm going to pay it back."

Mother: "Well, you better not be out there spending that money, givin' it to no damn man and you better not be out there spending it on no damn drugs."

Me: "Ma, I got a man to buy me drugs if I'm stupid enough to want them—where'd you come up with that?" Give money to a man? Shoot, they should be paying just for the privilege of our presence, Girlfriend!

As far as relatives are concerned, I think it's bad when you keep secrets in the family. Now, I'm not saying everybody has to know every little detail, even though it's more fun because then you find out what kind of nutcases you really have in your family.

I've had Girlfriends tell me horror stories about their meddling families. My advice to them goes like this:

Your family bothering you?

Relatives driving you nuts?

Move and don't leave a forwarding address!

I know this sounds drastic, but sometimes we need to be on our own, make our own choices, and just live our lives without any familial advice for a while.

One of the things that always bothered me before we came to California was how my family members took advantage of my husband's kindness and generosity.

Husband is really good at fixing things and putting things together. There was a time in our lives when he'd make the rounds to all of our relatives' houses on Christmas Eve and put together all the new bicycles and any other toy that was too complicated for dunderhead relatives to figure out. Finally I had to tell them all, "Excuse me, this is my man and I need him to help me." Once we moved to California the relatives' abuse vanished—you can't assemble a toy train-track when you are 2,000 miles away.

But I can't imagine being totally removed from my relatives, regardless of how strange and demanding they are. When my mother was living, we talked all the time. Yeah, I had big phone bills—still do—but it's worth it. The telephone company loves me! I had one call that lasted 444 mintes—shoot, I didn't think that even I could talk that long.

Family is family. You can't pick these people, you just have to deal with who they are and what they are. And you have no jurisdiction over their behavior.

On the other hand, your friends, like your husband, are the family that you do get to choose. They are all precious and you must always treat them with the respect that they deserve.

My brothers and sisters are always on me about being so generous with my friends. I tell them that it's because my friends treat me better. They respect me and value my time and energy. Now, how can you criticize that?

SO WHAT IS THIS MARRIAGE THING REALLY ALL ABOUT?

Yeah, yeah, you think the honeymoon is over. But that's only in your mind because if you work on it you can keep your marriage full of fun and life. In any situation, joy is where you make it.

Marriage is about growing together. I am amazed that Husband has consistently been nice to me all these years. How gracious he still is. How he defends me. How he understands my outrageous personality (sometimes).

Being in show business may seem like a hard job to some people, but I don't have the hardest job. My husband has the hardest job. It takes a good man to stand back and watch his wife take center stage, especially when he's done so much of the leg work.

Yeah, Husband has the hardest job because ultimately his job is to keep me calm and happy. When he keeps me happy I can go out and keep the world happy. We're a team and it takes the two of us to make Mother Love her best.

I have respect for him as a man.

I have respect for him as my husband.

I have respect for him as the head of my household.

I have respect for him because he is the father of my wonderful son. And even after all these years, my husband never ceases to amaze me. Recently we had this conversation:

Me: "Ain't you tired of me?"
Husband: "No."

141

Me: "Why do you stay here with me?"
Husband: "You make me very happy. . . ."

I had never heard him say this before.
It just popped out of his mouth after all these years.
It's these little things that keep a marriage going.
These brief moments of matrimonial miracles.

Oooo, Girlfriend. Ain't these the two finest lookin' men you've ever seen? And they're mine.

My masterpiece.

But only together is the picture complete.

CHAPTER EIGHT

*I remember when Mama put rocks in your pocket to
keep you from flying over the fence.*
—My Sister

❤ ❤ ❤

When I was a little kid I was just skin and bones and
everyone would tease me because I couldn't gain weight.
The boys used to say, "If you punch her in the eye she'll
look like a needle."

When the wind came off of Lake Erie it would pick
me up and blow me onto the nearest fence. Or even worse,
I'd get caught up in a tree.

Across the street from our house was a special school
for deaf kids. Sometimes the wind would snatch me, carry
me across the street, and throw me up onto the fence. My
brothers and sisters would leave me there, dangling in the
wind, and make fun of me.

They'd complain to Mother on a regular basis:

"Mama, we can't take her noplace. She's on the fence
again!"

"Oh, Lord, Mama, she's stuck up in a tree!"

But worst of all was the community pool. A few kids had drowned from climbing the wall to sneak in a swim, so for safety reasons the top of the wall was embroidered with curled barbed wire. Once I got caught in all that curled barbed wire and I couldn't get down. Nobody would help me as the boys walked by and looked up under my dress. It was during this humiliating moment that I learned never to show anyone that you're embarrassed because people will just take advantage of you.

My mother's solution to all of this? She sewed big patch pockets inside my car coat and filled them with rocks to anchor me. And I had to wear saddle shoes instead of those little patent leather numbers—anything and everything to ground me! Otherwise I'd be airborne.

145

This didn't do much for my self-esteem, but Mother told me that it was important to have confidence about yourself no matter what. So I might have carried rocks in my pocket and worn heavy saddle shoes, but I always wore really pretty dresses and Mama took me to the beauty school every two weeks to get my hair done. Those extra things that mother did for me anchored me.

I really was a funny-looking kid. I was very dark-skinned but I had real red undertones. Got this from my daddy. He was fair skinned with red hair.

Daddy?

Yeah, I had a daddy until I was nine. As a member of the Sea Dragons, my daddy was one of the first Black scuba diver in America. But he was a large man who drank, smoked, ate a high-fat diet, and didn't take very good care of himself. He was hospitalized for hypertension when he weighed 345 pounds, and he died in the strangest way.

He was sitting on the toilet in a hospital ward, pants down around his ankles, telling a joke. Before he reached the punch line he started laughing so hard that he died. It was a massive coronary that killed him.

The hospital didn't know what to do. For two days they didn't notify my mother. How do you call a woman, thirty years old with six children, and say, "We're sorry to tell you that your husband is dead"?

Well, now you know the next question has got to be, "Well, how'd he die?"

The answer?

"Well he died sittin' on the toilet with his shorts down, telling a man a joke, and fell over dead when he got to the punch line."

This was not something that was going to be easy to tell someone. He died February 15 and we didn't find out about his death until the seventeenth. One of my mother's friends who lived in the front row of the projects had heard about it and came to my mother to offer her condolences. My mother hadn't heard about it yet. This woman had gone so far over the edge in her grief that my mother thought she was talking about her own husband.

And then she said, "Oh, I'm so sorry, I'm so sorry, Shirley. . . ." My mother was like, What are you tripping out about? Then she realized it was Daddy who was gone and, boy, she was mad! How could he leave her to take care of six children?

Yeah, that was my daddy. A little colorful family history. Speakin' of color, when you're colored (I prefer being called colored to being called Black), it's difficult to determine exactly what color you are.

My solution as a child? Well, I got out my crayons and tried each one on my skin until I found a color that blended perfectly. According to Crayola crayons, I am

Burnt Sienna. In the summertime I turn to Crayola's Navy Blue. To this day these are my colors.

And when I was thirteen the most magical thing happened: I went to bed skinny and flat-chested and woke up as a 36B-cup overnight. Not only did I have breasts, I had wide breasts just like that!

When I started dating, one boy told me I had pretty breasts and would ask me to take off my shirt and bra so that he could marvel at their magnificence! From this moment on I realized how easy it would be to please a man.

But wait a minute, Girlfriend! I'm supposed to tell you how to be a better parent and help you become a better parent. What has all of the above got to do with this? Self-esteem.

From the moment your child can look in the mirror and say, "Hi!" he or she should feel good about themselves. One of the most important lessons to teach our children is how they can feel comfortable about who they are and what they look like when they walk out that big front door. So what if cute five-year-old Tammy has a big fat butt? She should always be made to feel that it's a really nice fat butt.

When I was a camp counselor lots of little kids were confused about their knobby knees, their curly hair, and whether they were too tall or too short. I taught them an exercise that I did as a child and still teach my friends as grown women.

It's simple. Get a piece of paper and draw a self-portrait. Without a doubt we all draw ourselves looking worse than we really are. Thank God that God is a far better artist than you or I because drawing yourself honestly is really tough. When I drew my self-portrait and held it up to the mirror next to my real face, my whole attitude

147

changed. I was seventeen, and from that point on I realized that I was okay. Suddenly all of my "Oh God!"s vanished. The chick I saw in the mirror was a hell of a lot better looking than the face on the paper.

ENCOURAGING YOUR CHILDREN TO USE THEIR GOD-GIVEN TALENTS

As kids we used to get up Sunday morning and entertain my mother. My brother and I would get up and dance and sing and then my two sisters and I would sing this silly song called "The Three Bears." Mother's friends would come over and pay us five dollars apiece to do this number. This was the first time I ever got paid for performing. My mother's friends loved to come over and see three big, broad, chicks like us singing "The Three Bears." By the time we finished the song she would be on the floor screaming with laughter as she handed five bucks to each of us.

Then she'd point to me and scream, "Go get that girl! Go get that girl! She's so funny!" I'd entertain them some more. When we got to be teenagers, Mother said, "I don't want this to be the devil's workshop, so I got something for you all to do."

It was "culture time." Yeah, we may have lived in the projects, but we were very, very cultured. We went to camp, Bible school, were the first kids in the project to brag about the color television, a stereo, and bunk beds.

One of my mother's best short speeches was:

"The world is your back door. Go out and play. Go out and jump on it! Go out and kick the world's ass and let them know that you were here!"

And that's what I've always done. I've let them know that I was here. For all the fights, my mother gave me my moral framework. She gave me my direction and kicked me in the butt as she sent me on my way. As much as she cursed me, she loved me for my gumption. Yeah, love your kids with everything you got, but be tough with them because the world is a very tough place.

THE IMPORTANCE OF FAMILY—FOR THE SAKE OF YOUR KIDS

Families come in all shapes, sizes, and colors. I was taught that family is where you go and they have to let you in. If you teach this to your children, no matter what happens in their lives, I truly believe that they will eventually come home. Then you can deal with the problems, however bad they are.

149

When the news came that my daddy had died, my auntie and uncle were with us. The two family drunks were the most sober ones in the bunch helping us through this difficult time. And I, as a young girl, truly appreciated their help.

Eventually my auntie ended up in the hospital, dying of cancer. She and my mother were ever so close, and of course I felt like their shadow. Mother told me that I had to go with her to see Auntie. On the way to the hospital we stopped at the Red Devil Barbecue, which sold the hottest barbecue in town. This stuff was so hot that you could only eat it if you were really, really drunk and you could only pass it out if you were drunk. This stuff could set your butt on fire and have you running around with your whole butt flaming. Mama told me we were gonna get some of their pork-shoulder sandwiches and that I should put some extra sauce in my pockets.

We snuck it into the hospital and up to the common

ward where my Auntie was. There was no privacy. It was
just awful! Well, we had Auntie up, here she is a cancer
patient, eating barbecued pork-shoulder sandwiches, which
she thought were the best.

She beat the cancer, came home from the hospital,
and then somebody robbed her for her Social Security
check. They killed her when they hit her on the head with
a brick. My mother was devastated. I was devastated and
confused.

After all Auntie had been through, to this day I don't
know why the good Lord took her. But I know we did right
by bringing her those pork-shoulder sandwiches. It helped
Auntie feel that she was a person, not just a hospital number, and I'm convinced that those pork-shoulder sandwiches
cured her cancer!

150

MY FIRST PROM

When I was a senior in high school, my mother bought
my class ring, she ordered my announcements, my year-
book, my prom dress, but, oh Lord, the prom! What a com-
motion that caused. Mother wanted me to go to the prom
with some little boy from school and I wanted to go with
this man.

Mother said, "I ain't paying for you to go nowhere
with no damn man. You are a high school senior and you
will go with a high school senior. You are not going with
some guy in a Biscuit Head military outfit to no prom. Forget it!"

When the little guy came to the door to pick me up
I was standing there with my red and white hot pants beneath my formal gown, hair done, makeup looking just fine,

and I said to him, "I have a headache. I'm not going." Slammed the door straight in his face.

Poor kid. Took his mother to the prom and came back and took me to the "after prom." *I should have listened to my mother.*

When we were grown up, the same guy tried to sue me for not marrying him because I told him when I was fourteen that I would marry him when he turned twenty-one. He came down to Ohio State in December and said, "Okay, you'll be twenty-one in two weeks. Here's your engagement ring."

I had totally forgotten about this guy, who arrived at my door in one of those "Flintstone" cars—no bottom to it, full of snow. He could have blown up on his drive down! And here he is telling me that we're going to get married and he's taking me back to Montana.

I told him, "Ain't no Black people in Montana. I'm not going with you—are you crazy?"

Two weeks later he had a lawsuit against me with the papers delivered to my mama's door: *You are hereby summoned to appear in court for breach of promise.*

Yes, he did. I couldn't believe it. Tell your children never to promise to marry someone when they are fourteen years old. *Never,* because they can hold you to it. In fact, never promise anyone anything because if they are determined, and get the right attorney, they'll come after you and sue your big behind with a smokin' gun! Now, I've had some bizarre relationships with men, but this one was really weird. Two fourteen-year-olds promising to marry and one holding the other to this juvenile promise? Excuse me!

ALWAYS TEACH YOUR CHILDREN

For all of her godliness, my mother could outcuss any sol-
dier. And she would cuss us out with such complicated
words that we'd have to look them up in the dictionary.

"Well, heck, Ma, what's that mean?"

"Look it up."

"Well, how do you spell it?"

She'd give us the first three letters and leave the rest
to us. From her I learned that there are many, many, many
ways to teach children—even with profanity!

Every room in our house had a dictionary, and you
could say "Roget's Thesaurus" before you were six. And you
had to know how to use a thesaurus.

We were the only family in the projects who had a
set of encyclopedias. We had study time at the kitchen
table, and our friends were allowed to study with us—but
no talking. It was so quiet you could hear a rat pee on
cotton.

Everybody in the projects knew one another, gave to
each other, helped especially the sick and the elderly. We
had to scrub their floors and take out their trash, write
letters for them, and walk them to the grocery store. As
children we were taught to help whoever we could whenever we could.

My mother made it her job to take us to the museums
and on other educational field trips. Whenever the other
kids in the projects saw us pile into the car they'd shout,
"Oh! Oh! Oh! They're goin' on a field trip! They're leavin'—
hurry, let's go!" However many extra kids could fit in could
come. Sometimes the car would fill up with the other kids
before we had a chance to get in. Mama would tell them,
"You-all got to get out of the car because my babies have

gotta go, but whatever space is left can be for the rest of you.

THE REALITY OF THE NINETIES FAMILY

Nobody cooks anymore, but I still throw down. You can see me: I certainly do not miss a meal. And I'm glad to feed anyone who comes through my front door.

My son's friends love to come over because I make a big fuss over them. But in my house there are to be no hats, no foul language, and their pants might sag but they better pull them up when they enter my house.

I tell them, "You better speak to everybody you didn't spend the night with!"

And so it's "Good evening, everyone, how are you?" They are perfect gentlemen in my home and if we go out in public their mothers can't believe their behavior.

My attitude?

Well, I ain't gonna be afraid of some Biscuit Head child that don't pay rent nowhere. No way! Nope! And gang members?

I was with a bunch of gang members one day (somebody had to be with them). They were upstairs smoking and I told them, "I can't take all those cigarettes—put them out!"

It was amazing. These kids just looked at me. I said, "Don't make me take my shoe off. . . ."

Well, just like that they were putting them out in their hats.

> Me: "What you doin' walkin' around here with
> a bandana and a plastic bag on your
> head? Get that off of your head!"

They took those bags off and started in. "We're sorry, Mother Love. We're sorry. Oh—we're so sorry!"

Me: "Shut up! Boy, get that gum out of your mouth!" I put out my clean hand and let them put their spitty gum in my hand. I demanded that they clean off their faces.

Yes, they are children. They are not people to be mistreated and abused. They're small people who need to be nurtured and loved. You have to talk to them. And you have to tell them the same information over and over again until they get it. They can't process new information quickly, sometimes. It's not because they're stupid, they just need guidance and direction. They need to learn about boundaries. And we must teach them.

It is our responsibility as adults, all adults, responsible adults, to look out for all of our children. There are no differences in any children. They are all the same.

When the boys run away from home they always come to my house and I gotta call their mamas and tell them where they are. They're not evil, just confused. I see them as good boys who can turn into good men. They feel my attitude. And they respond in a positive manner.

The greatest joy I have is when people call me and tell me, "Your son is such a gentleman. He opens doors for ladies." He listens to his little girlfriends who he goes to school with. They are always calling him up, looking for advice and everything. They think he's so cool; maybe because his mom is Mother Love. (Then again, maybe not!)

FAMILY HUMOR

Sick humor runs in our family. Truly it does, and it must just pass along from one generation to the next. Look for it in yours.

When my son was five, Husband-to-be and I were living apart—yeah, I had bought him some new shoes. One morning my son and I were eating some cold Kentucky Fried Chicken that I had bought the night before.

I had a window in the kitchen that my son liked to look out of because he could see all the way down the street. As he stood on a milk crate, looking out the window, he reached for a piece of chicken from the stove. He took one bite out of it, and then threw it out the window!

❤

155

❤

"Wait a minute, boy! We're poor people! You don't be takin' a good piece of chicken and throwin' it out the window—what's wrong with you?" Then I gave him a strong whack on his little behind, and being the dramatic child he is, he fell to the floor, got up, and started singing with dance steps:

> I woke up in the mornin',
> I got a piece of chicken,
> I threw it out the window,
> My mama slapped me down,
> Pow!

He would then fall down on the floor.

"What kind of child are you? You don't get disciplined for throwing food out the window and then make up a song about it! Are you crazy?"

Do you know all day long all I heard was him singing

that song over and over again with him falling down on the floor? My mother-in-law-to-be heard him and thought I was abusing him. Of course Husband-to-be called me up and began questioning my parenting skills.

Girlfriend, even though my son has sung "The Chicken Song" and has his own Biscuit Head tendencies, I know I've done well by him. And there were a few years when I was a single parent.

Alone time seems to be the first thing you give up when you become both Mommy and Daddy. Without a doubt alone time is difficult to find when you're a single parent because your child or children always need something. I discovered that going to the bathroom provided a wonderful moment for some alone time. But my son figured out my strategy and would follow me in for a little conversation.

I'd say, "Well, why you in the bathroom? Mama's gotta go."

"Well, this is the only place I could get you still. This is the only place you not movin'. I want you to talk to me, Mommy."

He thought our bathroom was our place to confer. And it was always goofy stuff he needed to ask or tell me. In fact it was in the bathroom where my son learned how babies are made.

My son is now eighteen and still follows me into the bathroom. I close the door just in time.

I ask him:

"Can your problem wait until I finish?

"Can I pull my drawers up, baby?"

I'm only pretending that he's a nuisance—because no matter how old your children get, they will always need you. It's just different stages at different ages!

They're all Biscuit Heads, but I love 'em.

Girlfriend, don't you be forgettin' about my Auntie and her panty antics.

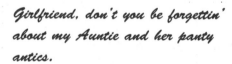

But don't forget the important stuff . . . like cheap lipstick sticks to your teeth.

CHAPTER NINE

❤ ❤ ❤

*C*elebrity!

Queen of advice on talk-show radio!

Makin' movies!

Hello, TV land!

Yeah, Girlfriend, Mother Love is everywhere!

She's fat-cat big-time livin' on easy street!

But guess what?

They ain't kiddin' when they say, "There's no business like show business." One minute you're Miss Fine Thing, all these show-biz folks ready to lick the soles of your shoes, and the next minute it's Mother Who? Mother What? And before you know it you're overdrawn at the bank, your pockets are empty, and your cash stash is gone. (I'm still trying to figure out if it was my Biscuit Head Husband or Dunderhead Son who found mine!)

But shoot, just about everybody I know and love has

been broke sometime in their life. From bus drivers, to teachers, to truck drivers, to writers, to computer consultants, to salespeople, to entertainers like me. Now, going broke ain't no picnic, but it ain't the end of the world, either.

Going broke happens for lots of reasons. A recession hits and your company is part of the fallout. Industries relocate or go out of business. They're cutting back on personnel. You're forced into early retirement. You become ill—and if you are in the entertainment industry, like me, you are at the mercy of producers and directors. I can't think of a definitive adjective that suits them!

The most important thing to remember is that if you did your job, whatever it was, to the best of your ability, then you've got nothing to be ashamed of. You might be broke, but at least you can still say your prayers when you go to bed and sleep in peace.

It wasn't that long ago when Husband, Son, and I went through a really rough money-crunch period. Husband wasn't working and Mother Love wasn't in demand. Since I never knew when a residual check was coming through, I couldn't make any promises to the creditors. We were two months behind on just about everything, and constantly negotiating with the telephone company so that they wouldn't disconnect us.

What did I do? I did what I had to do so that we could survive. I applied for unemployment benefits that I had never realized I was entitled to. When I found out that I was eligible for the highest amount they pay in the state of California, I felt like we would be okay—that is until I found out it was only $230 a week!

But having been a poor person almost all my life, during this period my family didn't fall apart. We didn't lose

159

our faith. Our circumstances would change, and for the time being we felt that getting something was better than nothing.

Girlfriend, living on $230 a week is no easy feat! I pinched here and there, truly "robbing Peter to pay Paul," keeping the creditors at bay.

Let me tell you, Girlfriend, the most humbling experience I've had in the seventeen years I've been in show business, since I've been Mother Love, was sitting in the Welfare office applying for food stamps while signing autographs. Everyone there thought I was doing some exposé on the Welfare Department.

Mother Love on Welfare? No way! No, she's here to help cheer up all us poor people who are feeling down and out.

Now, I'm sittin' there trying to get some food stamps so my big butt don't miss no meal. Poor people can really relate to this because when you can't pay your rent or your bills, at least you know you can eat. This is why so many poor people are big. We can eat and we know how to make food stretch. When you're living in the projects or some other low-rent place, you can't afford to go out and buy a car—but you can afford to buy a big pot roast, potatoes, carrots, and cornmeal. At least you can eat well.

When you're poor, food becomes your comfort. My mother fed us pork chops, applesauce, fried potatoes, and grits for breakfast. Now, it's not like we needed all this food because we had to go out and plow forty acres, chop wood, and bale hay. Heck, there was no way we could even walk all that food off because our school was right around the corner! And when that heavy meal hit I couldn't concentrate and would be fallin' asleep in the classroom.

Where does Mother Love find herself years later?

Welfare office. Somewhere, deep down inside, I'm thinking, This ain't right. But, well, we ain't got no money—but we can eat. I ain't gonna let us go hungry!

I'm sitting in the Welfare office, waiting for my name to be called, and people who recognize me are comin' over, saying, "Hey, Mother Love—how ya doin'? You here undercover to tell the truth about Welfare?"

> Me: "No . . ."
> Welfare recipient: "Will you autograph my
>   health card? Will you autograph my food-
>   stamp card—this is an old one, so I'm
>   gonna keep it 'cause I'm here to get a new
>   one."

161

When my name was called, the Welfare lady had taken care of everybody else. She was pleased that I had filled out the application correctly and completely. . . .

> Welfare lady: "Before you leave you have got
>   to give me your autograph. My husband
>   just loves you. We miss you on the
>   radio."

I didn't know whether I should be happy that she recognized me or sad that I had to be sitting in the Welfare office. But I was glad that there was someplace for me to go when things got bad, when we didn't have jobs.

Yeah, it's embarrassing to admit this, but it's very real. It's what I had to do. But the fact that I knew that I couldn't live on Unemployment and food stamps motivated me to keep trying, to keep going, to keep telling myself, "I can do better than this."

I was blessed that I only had to rely on Welfare for two months in the summertime. This is the hardest time for many working actors unless you have a TV series. Acting jobs seem to vanish, and you just have to struggle through it.

I've worked harder in show business in California than I ever did in Cleveland, Ohio. Every moment you have to keep on trying, trying to keep it all going and trying to keep on a happy face. There are times when I have been on television in borrowed clothes, when I've owed the hairdresser for doing my hair and the manicurist for doing my nails.

162

We all got our good times and we all got our bad times. It's a matter of making the conscious choice to survive. I am no different from anybody else. I was born and raised in the projects, came from a poor family, and was raised by a single mother. But I wanna give a big kick in the booty to those woebegone people who do nothing but complain. Unfortunately, many people living in poverty feel they must stay in poverty.

> Woebegone: "Oh, woe is me. . . . I can't do
> this. . . . Oh, I ain't educated. . . ."
> Me: "Take yourself back to school. Take
> advantage of the free training programs
> offered by the Welfare Department."
> Woebegone: "Oh, I can't get no job. . . ."
> Me: "Well, get yourself job-ready. Prepare
> yourself."

I don't care if the only job you can get is to pick up crap with a splinter. At least you can be proud that you've got a job.

Woebegone: "Well, I ain't gettin' off of Welfare
        just to work at McDonald's."
Me: "Well, excuse me! But you have children
        who look up to you as their role model.
        Don't you think it's good that they see
        you go to work instead of sitting on the
        sofa all day?"

I have Girlfriends whose mothers were on Welfare and now they're on Welfare. They had kids when they were teenagers. Now their teenage daughters have babies and they're on Welfare. That's three generations of Welfare.

My reaction? This ain't my kind of party! I am out of here and will not be involved in this.

Their reaction? That I thought I was better than everybody else.

No, babies, Mother Love can't stay on Welfare. This ain't for me. I want a better life for me, I want a better life for my son, I want a better life for my family.

Once you're hung up in the system, it's tough to get out. But I want you to know that there is a way out. There are so many places within the Welfare system where you can go that will help you get out. But you have to make the effort, and education is the key.

I remember growing up and how I could not imagine that someone in my neighborhood could not read. If they couldn't read we tutored them and helped them so that they could. It's beyond my reality to believe that we have over twenty million functional illiterates in our country.

There are always going to be people who are poor.

There are always going to be people who don't know. Just make sure you ain't one of them.

I remember this great big Black Baptist minister who

was popular during the '60s and '70s. Reverend Ike was flamboyant and flashy, with his diamond rings and Cadillac, and he was one of the first televangelists.

Reverend Ike would come on TV, spewing his fire and brimstone, and would always say, "The best way to help poor people is not to be one of them!"

And I live by that. If I'm gonna help poor people, the first thing I gotta do is not be a poor person. How am I not going to be poor? I gotta be educated. I gotta be smart. Just because I came from poverty doesn't mean that's where I'm going. Poverty was my history, it is not my destiny. And it is this way of thinking that gets me and my family through a financial crisis.

DEALING WITH ILLNESS AND HELPLESS RELATIVES

Remember when Auntie had cancer and we snuck those pork-shoulder sandwiches into the hospital? Yeah, she enjoyed the sandwiches, but what was more important was that we spent quality time with her. We read to her, we played cards with her, and we told silly jokes as we laughed with her.

Auntie would whisper in my ear, "Go over there and bother that doctor. Go on, girl, and give him a hard time 'cause he's working on my nerves."

In my family, when somebody is ill you don't just turn them over to the medical profession. The same is true with the elderly. We would never think of putting my eighty-eight-year-old great-grandmother into a nursing home. Well, mostly because she got kicked out of three of them.

So we had to take her in. Was she grateful?

Great-Grandmother: "I don't wanna live with none of y'all! You don't do what I want ya to do!"

What did she expect from us before she moved in? She expected us to come to her apartment and scrub the iron steps, scrub the concrete, and sweep the dirt.

My father was still alive when he and my mother decided to bring Great-Grandmother to our house to live. And she had her own room.

We'd all protest: "Why we got to have her live here with her old self? Why we got to comb that nappy blue hair of hers?"

Yeah, Great-Granny had blue hair. After it turned white she had it rinsed blue. And combing her hair was like combing steel wool.

It was long.

It was thick.

It was wiry—and to make it worse, she was tender-headed!

She could not stand for her hair to be combed, but she wanted it to be combed all the way through to its very end. When you washed her hair it just matted up like a big cotton ball on her head.

We had to use this old, thick-toothed comb and comb it in sections. If any of her hair came out she'd start screamin', "You're pullin' my hair out! You're pullin' my hair out! Get away from me!" Then she'd start smackin' whoever she could reach. It was a nightmare. But we couldn't put her off on anybody else.

My father said that we needed the influence of our great-grandmother, that we should know and respect our elders.

Excuse me?

165

Now here was a woman who chewed tobacco, smoked cigarettes, and dipped snuff. She could spit forty feet, without any of it dripping, straight into a spittoon. And she didn't use her spittoon just to catch her spit. She did all of her "business" in it and demanded that we empty it. Didn't matter to her that her bedroom was right next to the bathroom!

As far as I can remember she was eighty-eight her entire life. So she had to be about 112 when she finally died in her sleep. Why, she outlived my father!

We were taught that when someone was sick or going through hard times, you automatically entertained them or played with them. If someone was hospitalized they had a visitor every day. Regardless of who (and how unbearable they were), what, or why the crisis, our family always pulled together.

I have a Girlfriend whose mother has cancer. She gets sicker by the day and probably will die before this book is published. Now get this: Because of some kind of crap that happened in the past, her brothers and sisters who live only minutes away rarely go to see her and rarely call her up. They live in Dallas and Girlfriend lives in California. Girlfriend calls her mother every day, sends her cards, school pictures of her grandchildren, and flowers twice a month. She can't leave California because of her husband's job, but she does everything she can think of to make her mother's life better for whatever time she has left. Girlfriend is very upset with her brothers and sisters and we talk about what she can and can't do.

How does Mother Love feel about this? For any of you to abandon your mother like that, knowing she has very little time left, is a disgrace. I don't care about the crap of the past. This is your mother, the only mother you have on the face of the planet. You mean to tell me that you're not mature enough to put the past behind you and look out for your mother?

Girlfriend will fly home for the funeral, of course, and I've told her how her brothers and sisters will act. They'll be the ones whoopin' and hollerin' and crying a river of tears over the coffin. But not out of sorrow. Out of guilt!

My mother dropped dead sitting on the edge of her bed at her house, with her children, her grandchildren, her brother, and her friends in the house. This is the way it's supposed to be. I can't imagine my brothers and sisters not talkin' to my mother or not being there for her. Now, I wasn't talkin' to my sisters and brothers at this time, but I sure as hell was talking to my mother all the time.

Mother: "Can't you just get past all of that
with your brothers and sisters? Can't you
just forget it and move on?"
Me: "Well, yeah, Mama, for your sake I'll get
past it because I want you to be happy. It
ain't that serious that I can't speak to
them."

When my mother passed away and I came home for the funeral, the whisper at the wake was, "Oooooh, we won't see her no more. She's gonna go back to California and ain't gonna be calling any of us. They probably can't wait to get away from here. . . ."

I used to tell my mother that if God chose to take her before me, rest assured that if I didn't have to deal with them I wouldn't. But my mother would remind me that not only were they my sisters and brothers, but they were the only sisters and brothers I had. Good, bad, indifferent, right or wrong, the six of us have a major connection: we are all our mother's children.

I wouldn't want to see anything bad happen to them. And I wouldn't break my neck to help some of them, because some of them are not nice people. But if something serious happened to them I'd be the first one to take care of them and their kids—and do whatever I had to do.

RELATIVES GETTIN' READY TO MOVE IN?

Whoa, Girlfriend! Let them know as soon as their feet land on your doormat that they're staying with you on a limited basis, for just a short period of time.

I let both of my brothers live with me and I'd never make that mistake again. I let two of my sisters live with me and I'd never make that mistake again. Because when the relatives move in they want to take over!

Here are some things to watch out for when Brother, Sister, Cousin, or Uncle come for an "extended visit":

• Don't let them start changing your household rules.

• Don't let them run up your phone bill (you may want to consider installing a separate line for a visiting relative).

• No matter how often they ask, don't loan them money.

• Don't let them use your car unless your insurance covers other drivers.

• Let them go grocery shopping with you and don't say no when they ask if they can chip in.

• It's not okay for sexy Sister, Cousin, or Girl-friend to be walking around your house in her bra and panties.

• When you're cleaning your house give them chores to do, too.

• If they're not working, let them cook dinner. Everybody's got to pull their weight.

When their time is up don't hesitate to let them know. Of course you should give them a week's notice.

♥
169
♥

CRISIS AND YOUR MARRIAGE

A life crisis can make your marriage stronger if you and Husband can stand together, tall and strong. While the strength of one is great, the strength of the two of you is greater.

But sometimes a crisis destroys a marriage. I know a Girlfriend and her husband who were married ten years before they had any kids. When they had their baby he was born with spinal meningitis. Husband couldn't deal with it and left Girlfriend and her very sick baby. Just plain walked away. When the baby died Husband flipped out and came back.

Me: "Well, what you here for now? You've been here with this woman for ten years, y'all finally have a baby, the baby has

meningitis, they tell you the baby will
die—and you can't even stick around and
be by your wife?"

Him: Silence.

Me: "You're a punk! You left her here to grieve
by herself."

Him: "Well, I was grieving too. . . ."

Me: "Well, you're supposed to be with her. It
was your baby too! How could you go off
and leave her?"

While he was gone, Girlfriend fell completely to pieces—
and what Girlfriend wouldn't if she lost her baby, her man,
and her marriage in one fell swoop! She started doing drugs
and went crazy for about two years before she finally came
to her senses. She's worked hard to put her life back together again, and last I heard she had found herself a very
nice boyfriend.

Life is full of crises. And you can't just walk away
when one hits. It's easy to be a good person when life is
going according to your plan. But the true test of who you
are and what you're made of is when it starts raining crap
big-time! Some of the things that can happen:

Family member gets sick with a terminal illness.

A relative commits suicide, leaving three little kids behind.

You lose your job.

Your child gets into drugs.

Your daughter gets pregnant at fifteen and she doesn't
know who the father is.

Your home is destroyed in a fire, flood, or earthquake.

This list is endless. At any time, in any place, something terrible can happen.

What does Mother Love do when it happens to her? I hang tough, do what I can to alleviate the crisis, and go to God. Keeping my head and my heart close to my maker in prayer while taking action is what has always gotten me through a crisis.

CHAPTER TEN

*God bless 'em! They're all just a bunch
of Biscuit Heads!*
—Mother Love

❤   ❤   ❤

*O*kay.

I got you ready to meet them.

Told you how to meet them.

Told you how to keep them.

Shared my wedding to show you that whatever can go wrong could go wrong . . . but you can and will rise above the occasion.

Told you how to keep the sizzle in sex, 'cause hey, Girlfriend, we like to make that "thang sang"!

Showed you that when living together is going to be forever, joy is where and when you make it.

I have given you some sound advice about raising your babies into decent men and women.

And shared my own Welfare story because going broke ain't the end of the world—look at me now, I'm doin' okay.

So, what's the truth about these Biscuit Head men who don't know where they're going or where they've been?

First thing you got to realize,

girlfriend,

Girlfriend,

GIRL-FRIEND!

is that you cannot raise a grown man. All his mama didn't do, you ain't gonna do. You cannot get a man and decide, Oh! I'm going to change him once we get into this deep, loving relationship.

No, you better work on changing yourself. You can't be sittin' there thinkin' about how you're going to get rid of that ugly outfit, that stupid outdated stereo, and that funky record collection of his. If that's what he likes, that's what he likes and should keep.

Love a man for who he is and what he is. Don't try to make him over. And if you're tempted to, think about how you would feel if someone came along and told you how you should change. It ain't gonna happen, Girlfriend. Accept him and yourself for who you are as individuals.

And what about Biscuit Head? What does he really want from you besides a decent meal, a clean house, a fun conversation (you be Big Ears, okay?), and some good lovin'?

He may not say it, or even consciously know it, but what he wants is for you to be vulnerable. He wants you to need him.

Men, by nature, protect, and women, by nature, nurture. And men want to protect those who nurture them. These feelings are primitive and instinctive. They can't be changed. To try to change them is to go against human nature. This is why many tough, strong, successful women,

173

who rarely show their vulnerability, may seem less appealing.

Girlfriend's got this big job, makes all this money, is a fashion queen (in fact she taught the fashion police everything they know!), drives a fat-cat car with no car payments, and has a fancy house or apartment to come home to. But the only sound she hears when she opens the door is her own echo or the roar of her cat. If she's not into cats she probably has birds or a dog who she dresses up in fancy coats and rhinestone collars and spoon-feeds gourmet meals. Heck, I know Girlfriends who take better care of their pets than they would any man. What man, biscuit head and all, is going to want to feel that he comes second after the dog?

Girlfriend, if you think you can get more love and fulfillment from a pet than a man, then you are just being bitter, angry, and have obviously been hurt by men in the past. Yeah, you can keep the pet, but feed it a one-course meal. Save your slavin' over the stove for that nice man you meet. Feed *him* the twelve-course meal!

Most all of us can play the rock-hard woman, but Biscuit Head don't want that. He wants someone who's going to show him that she feels safe with him. That there is something special about him that only he has, and that she has to have.

As much jumping up and down, screamin', and rantin' and ravin' that I do, my Biscuit Head husband knows that for me there is no man who smells, or tastes, or feels as good as he does. As I've said before, he's my second skin. And I make sure he knows this.

For Mother Love there is nothing like being able to be collected in a hug in my husband's arms, to lay my head on his shoulder, and for him to say to me, "Baby, don't worry. It's gonna be all right. I'll make it all right for you. . . ."

Now, I know damn well that I can take care of myself. And I can take care of him and our son if I have to. But Biscuit Head Husband's logic is the best:

"You can take care of us and I can take care of us— so we know we're gonna be all right."

Now, what makes more sense than that?

No, Biscuit Head Husband is not a big verbal guy with flowers and kisses all over. But I just know that he is willing to direct his life so that my life is okay, to tell me that he will do whatever he can. Shoot, how can I not be vulnerable to that?

Girlfriend, remember:

Biscuit Head men don't think like we think.

They don't feel like we feel.

They don't feel what we feel.

And they don't communicate like Girlfriends.

You know how you can sit around and talk to your Girlfriend about anything: compare the size of your tits, talk about getting a "lift," and it ain't no big thing. Well, you ain't gonna see guys sharing these details about themselves. Why? Because they're too insecure. And it's just not their way.

Girlfriends will always be able to communicate better with one another than with their men. We want them to communicate, but they don't communicate the same way we do. Men feel if they're there with you, at your side, that should be enough.

Yeah, but we wanna hear:

"Baby I love you.

"I think you're the finest thing on two feet.

"That outfit is slammin'.

♥

175

♥

"You're lookin' like I just wanna do it to you right now.

"We don't even have to go to the party—you're the best thing in the world!"

Girlfriend, if this is what you expect you are living in a fantasy. Come on back! Let me reel you on in. C'mon, Girlfriend!

This is where we're supposed to be. You wanna be involved with one of these Biscuit Head men, and God bless 'em, we love them dearly—but they are Biscuit Heads.

No, they don't know where their belongings are. I mean when was the last time you said to Husband or Boyfriend, "Honey! Have you seen my black panties? I can't find my red bra." Probably never. And even if you asked, he don't know.

Now, if Biscuit Head can't find his other blue sock or yellow shirt or paisley tie, you're gonna hear about it. You better know where that sock, shirt, and tie are.

No, men are not like women. They don't think like us, look like us, act like us, sound like us, talk like us, feel like us. Conversely, thank God for Jesus that women ain't like men!

I wouldn't wanna be a man. And I'm not that much into this women's-lib thing because I've always been a liberated woman. I've always been able to stand on my own two feet. I've always been able to work and take care of myself. I haven't had to depend on a man to do any of those things for me.

Yeah, love your Biscuit Head. And let him feel how much you love him and need him, all the while knowing that you can depend on yourself whenever you have to. Be compatible with your man. But don't be a problem to him, and don't let him be a problem to you. Like I told y'all earlier, don't ever get involved with somebody who's got more problems than you do. If he's got an ex-wife, a dog, kids, and alimony—well, you know that's gonna be a problem. If you can't handle it, then move on!

Life is too short to be riddled with problems you can't deal with—his or yours. And life is too short to waste with someone you're uncomfortable with and unhappy with, including *yourself*. If you're not happy with yourself, you ain't never gonna be happy with no man.

So the first thing you gotta do is work on yourself. You have to know what it is you want, what it is you wanna do, so that you can at least convey that to a man. And don't worry about whether or not he gets it, because at least you know.

❤

177

❤

Yeah, make him feel needed, but don't ever get yourself so wrapped up with one of these Biscuit Head men that you lose yourself—not with Husband, not with Child, not with Boyfriend. Always know who you are. And if you have any questions about yourself, it's time to stand back and find out the answers. Get with the program!

And you know, Girlfriend, when we're confused about ourselves or have some problems with ourselves, we usually dump it all on our Biscuit Head men. Sometimes Biscuit Head has done everything sweet and nice that he can, but what does he get from us?

"You don't love me enough!"

"You don't spend enough time with me!"

"You don't give me enough sex!"

Sex? That's a whole 'nother thing right there. Let me tell you about sex and these Biscuit Head men. . . .

The myth is that men think more about sex than women. This is a farce, at least to me because I think about sex all the time. I think about good sex, about how nice it is to have my hot husband all over me, or however we be. Yeah, he's my second skin.

Women think more about the quality of sex while men are more concerned with the conquest. This is the boyish quality of a Biscuit Head.

Did I say boy?

You gotta know the difference between a boy and a man because it's big. And one of the biggest mistakes women make is marrying immature boys, thinking they're men because they're forty, when they are not mentally prepared for the commitment.

I have a rule: Women don't belong with boys and men don't belong with girls. Women need men and girls need boys.

The only reason a forty-five-year-old woman is with a twenty-three-year-old boy is because he's got stamina and a harder body. Now, I'm not saying a twenty-three-year-old guy can't be a man. In fact, I know men who are eighteen years old.

My son is one, but we don't tell him that. Lord, would his head swell! At eighteen he's responsible for his actions and he respects women. He's not one to paw all over a girlfriend or pressure her into having sex. Now, I'm not saying he wouldn't like to get in her drawers, 'cause let's not be ridiculous. (My Biscuit Head son walks around with six and seven "jimmy hats" in his pocket—he's ready if she really feels ready.)

Why do we have so many grown boys in the world? Because many women didn't think they needed to have a positive male role model in their sons' lives who would help them change from boys to men. Yeah, some men leave on their own, but many are chased away by women who listen to their male-bashing mothers. As Mother used to say, "Men ain't no good. They just find you, jump in your underwear, and get rid of you."

My son is a man because I didn't listen to my mother. I know you can't teach what you don't know. So what woman walking on the face of this planet can teach a boy to be a man? None. He's got to learn that from another man.

It's from another man that he will learn to be a good husband and a good father.

But it's also from another man that he can learn to be a thug, drug dealer, and criminal. Why do you think gangs are so prominent? Unfortunately, young boys are learning from older boys about this kind of lifestyle. Once the older boys get them, they don't want to let them go. No matter what, hold on to your children and you (and hopefully your man) be the strongest influence in their lives.

If you're thinking of commitment with your Biscuit Head man, look to his father or whoever his role model was and is. Heck, men have been checking out our mothers for years to see what kind of women we'd be to grow old with! Do the same thing.

My husband saw his father go to work every day.

My husband saw his father bring home his paycheck every Friday and sign it over to his mother because she took care of the house and the bills.

My husband lived in a clean house and was well cared for with his brothers and sisters. Regardless of what happened behind closed doors, my husband saw his parents as a united couple.

My son sees his father go to work every day.

My son sees his father give me his paycheck every Friday.

My son lives in a clean house and is well cared for. He sees my husband and me as a united couple.

This is what my son will bring with him when he finds a woman he can open up to and share his emotions with. This is sacred love, love based on trust that should never be abused.

Girlfriend, when you find your Biscuit Head man who is ready to share his love and trust, don't look away. So what if he's a factory worker, garbageman, or drives a truck for UPS? Girlfriend, don't look away for someone "better." Stay focused and work with what you've already got.

No, Biscuit Head men don't babble like we do.

But sometimes the best answer is their answer:

"Yeah, baby. . . ."

When you find your Biscuit Head man, you be his Biscuit Head woman.

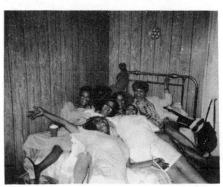

You need your Girlfriends to ride out those rough times . . .

. . . And thank God for Girlfriends!

Can you believe this skinny, one-bone chick wrote this book with me? Connie Church is the ultimate Girlfriend. (Photo: Eleanor Walker)

CONCLUSION

Baby, don't sweat the small stuff. And remember,
it's all small stuff.
—My Mother

♥   ♥   ♥

*T*he reason Mother Love continues to grow, expand, and flourish is because in life "real mother love" never leaves you. Girlfriend, not even in distance, not even after death.

As I grew up, my mother and I had a passionate love-hate relationship. Eventually our relationship grew into a genuine friendship. But I had to get all the junk out of me with my mother: the competition, the frustration, the anger. Sometimes she gave me great information. And lots of times she gave me hell.

> My mother: "You just use your head as a hat
>   rack!"
> I challenged her: "Why do you doubt your
>   parenting skills? Don't you think that
>   you've given me the right information?
>   Don't you think I can use it?"

My mother: "Heifer, get out of my house! You
   ain't gonna talk to me like that. . . ."

After this final confrontation we had no more problems between us. She eventually fessed up when I started
giving advice to the lovelorn. She said, "You know, I'm
really glad you didn't listen to me when it came to love.
And I'm glad you didn't take what I said about your Biscuit
Head husband seriously because he's a good man."

That was it. Our minds merged and we connected; we
became real Girlfriends.

My mother taught me to be bold, confident, and cu-
rious.

My mother whopped me when I tried to go toe-to-
toe with her.

My mother bailed me out when I was in trouble . . .
sometimes.

But beneath it all, whatever was happening didn't really matter.

It was all coming from her love.

From my mother's love.

I miss her so much.

❤   ❤   ❤

On the night my mother died I had a dream—and I knew
it was a dream, although it seemed very real. She came to
me in the dream and said, "You will remember everything
about this."

Girlfriend, she came up to the room I used to sleep
in when we lived in the projects. She was a big, huge shell
with no back and with her hair standing all over her head.
There was a light coming through her eyes, nose, and
mouth. She stretched out her arms, which were really big,
like they were swollen, put those big arms around me, and

said, "I am always here for you, no matter what, baby. You're gonna be okay. Don't fall apart. Don't let the rest of the children fall apart."

In my sleep I can always touch her and smell her.

And as I go through my life, I can see her in my own reflection.

Always tell your mother what you have to tell her, even if it means telling her off, because when she's physically gone she will continue to live in you and all the other people she leaves behind. Your "mother love" is your thread of wisdom that protectively winds around you and pulls you along through life.

Some of you Girlfriends may not have a mother. If not, seek another source for your dose of the comfort of "mother love." Maybe an auntie, your grandmother, or just a wise old Girlfriend. Whoever she is, Girlfriend, know that "mother love" is your partner for life.

It's not going to be all kisses and bubbles. But once you have found one another, your "mother love" will help you through the tough times in all of your relationships; it is your barometer for life.

Whether it's with your man, your children, a distant cousin, or your next-door Girlfriend, "mother love" will help you stand strong together as one.

Dang! Does anything really have to be that tough?

You don't pass judgment on anyone; you love them like they are. Yeah, we want our families to be better people—and that's only because we love them. "Mother love" means that we love each other for whatever we are and however we are. We have to find the connection, whatever it is.

A hobby.

A sport.

A conversation.

Even if it's only a smile. It doesn't take anything to smile at another human being.

Listen up, Girlfriends!

We don't have to be knocking each other in the head.

We don't have to be trying to take each other's husbands.

We don't have to mistreat our children because we feel bad about ourselves.

Why can't we all just say, "Hey, Girlfriend! How you doin'?"

—*Mother Love*

185